GLIMPSES
OF A
PUBLIC
IVY

GLIMPSES OF A PUBLIC IVY

50 Years at William & Mary

David L. Holmes

Edited by Susan Williamson
Illustrations by David Loebman

SCHIFFER
PUBLISHING

4880 Lower Valley Road · Atglen, PA 19310

Cover design by Chris Bower
Interior design by Mel Gallipeau at Incubate Design, LLC.
Type set in Novecento Slab and Marion Regular.
Cover photo courtesy of University Archives, Special Collections Research Center, William & Mary Libraries

ISBN: 978-0-7643-6444-0
Printed in India

Published by Schiffer Publishing, Ltd.
4880 Lower Valley Road, Atglen, PA 19310
Phone: (610) 593-1777; Fax: (610) 593-2002
Email: Info@schifferbooks.com, Web: www.schifferbooks.com

For our complete selection of fine books on this and related subjects, please visit our website at www.schifferbooks.com. You may also write for a free catalog.

Schiffer Publishing's titles are available at special discounts for bulk purchases for sales promotions or premiums. Special editions, including personalized covers, corporate imprints, and excerpts, can be created in large quantities for special needs. For more information, contact the publisher.

We are always looking for people to write books on new and related subjects. If you have an idea for a book, please contact us at proposals@schifferbooks.com.

To Timothy J. Sullivan

CONTENTS

The Sir Christopher Wren Building
is the oldest college building still
standing in the United States and an
iconic image of William & Mary.

INTRODUCTION

The College of William & Mary, founded in 1693, is America's second-oldest university. I joined its faculty in 1965 as an instructor in English. In 2013 I retired as the Walter G. Mason Professor of Religious Studies. During my forty-eight years at the university, I had the opportunity to teach outstanding students and to work with a wide variety of talented faculty and staff.

The following collection of vignettes, encompassing approximately fifty years, presents a kind of autobiography of William & Mary from the 1950s through 2000. It is not intended as a history of the university, since several well-written histories already exist. It is also not a personal essay. Rather, it is a different kind of writing. The fifty vignettes in the collection are based on fact, but the author has shaped and ordered the stories.

In recent years, scholars—led by a retired William & Mary English professor—have uncovered important and previously unknown information about Virginia's first college. Less research has been done about the life of William & Mary students, faculty, and alumni in later centuries. This book attempts to illuminate the important era in campus life and culture from 1950 to 2000. Separated into several sections, this book characterizes—generally with new information and sometimes with humor—the lives of undergraduates, graduates, faculty, administrators, and alumni. Because the vignettes were largely compiled via interviews, certain aspects of campus life may not be depicted in exacting detail. But such interviews can give a new perspective. They put readers into contact with fresh information they might not receive from a more scholarly book or journal article.

Various readers have encouraged the writing of these vignettes in the first person, but I have resisted. Although good reasons as well as ample precedents exist for writing in the third person, an explanation is in order. Above all, there is the overriding question of anonymity. Close to seventy persons contributed their memories of William & Mary to this book. Over a dozen of those contributors requested not to be identified. The alumna who looked back on how she chose William & Mary, the first Black Phi Beta Kappa, the alumni who contributed memories of college life such as "The Early Morning Class"—they and others welcomed the opportunities to share their memories. But over a dozen of the contributors asked not to be identified. The general who drove from the Pentagon to protest his son's grade, the alumna who worked secretly for the CIA, the professor who continually raided campus dumpsters to recycle discarded paper, the alumnus who was in jail when he should have been appearing in a theater production, the professors who gained reputations for eccentricity and absentmindedness, and finally the chair who accused a department member of poorly teaching a course the member did not even teach—none wanted to be identified.

"Look, it's a great story, but I'd find it immensely embarrassing if I were named," one alumnus declared.

Following a detailed interview, a professor stated, "You can use this material, but don't name me. I don't want to be viewed as a complainer."

Another faculty member declared, "Well, if you print that story and attribute it to me, I can think of two colleagues who will immediately become lifelong enemies."

After hearing such concerns, I realized that anonymity would be essential for this study of William & Mary history and life. The stories needed to be told, but some of the participants would not share them if their names were revealed. Ultimately, I found that anonymity had its strengths. Above all, it allowed the story to be told without fear of repercussions. When the interviewees for the vignettes in this book learned their identities would be protected, they became more candid and forthright.

For much the same reasons, all of the vignettes in this book are written in the third person. In reflecting on the times, I found it helpful to remove myself from the story. This is, after all, a collection of stories about life at the College of William & Mary, not about my life. Writing the stories in third person was not difficult. A number of authors have written autobiographies and nonfiction narratives in the third person. Jill Christman's award-winning *Darkroom: A Family Exposure* (2011) is a third-person narrative. Edward William Bok's third-person memoir, *The Americanization of Edward Bok: The Autobiography of a Dutch Boy Fifty Years After*, won the Pulitzer Prize in 1921. A long article in volume 9 of New Literary History[1] declares that the third person is used in "highly coded genres, such as historical memoirs ... in which the author slips himself into the place of a heterodiegetic narrator" (whatever that may be). The article cites such examples as Henry Adams's *The Education of Henry Adams*, Norman Mailer's *The Armies of the Night*, Truman Capote's *In Cold Blood*, Tom Wolfe's *Electric Kool-Aid Acid Test*, and Gertrude Stein's *The Autobiography of Alice B. Toklas*. All of these works have used the third person to tell their story effectively.

A university is a collection of students, staff, and educators—all seeking knowledge, enlightenment, fulfillment, and connection. The following vignettes include extraordinary achievement, humorous incidents, unique characters, and day-to-day life in a historic university located in an equally historic setting. This book is a narrative of people, places, and institutions navigating the second half of the twentieth century. In its vignettes, many readers will find duplicates of their own experience.

I. STUDENT LIFE AT WILLIAM & MARY

1. Three Alumni and Life at William & Mary

What was life like at the College of William & Mary in the 1950s? Memories of three alumni paint a picture of the era. Caucasian, middle class, academically earnest, and sometimes gifted, predominantly from Virginia, Protestant in religious background; these alumni were fairly typical William & Mary students for the times.

From the eighteenth century on, Virginia had always supplied the largest number of students to William & Mary. By the 1950s the largest number of freshmen came from the Virginia suburbs of Washington, DC. In 1950, one of these alumni was a woman student from Alexandria who was accepted to both Duke and William & Mary. Her father told her to choose William & Mary. She did, for "in those days," she declared in an interview, "a girl did what her father said." Today she recalls excellent teaching spread over four years, an enjoyable sociology major, panty raids (an occasional event on 1950s campuses), pledging a sorority that had a reputation for inclusiveness, and being "campused" (confined to her dorm, except for classes) after riding in a car without permission. Following her graduation, she worked for the CIA until she married an undergraduate classmate who had gone on to take a degree at William & Mary's Marshall-Wythe School of Law. She became a licensed clinical social worker and was in private practice for thirty years, doing marriage, family, and individual psychotherapy.

The second alumnus from the 1950s was raised in a prosperous neighborhood of Detroit. As a senior in high school, he expressed a desire to attend Dartmouth College. His father, however, was unwilling to pay Dartmouth's substantial tuition when Michigan's state universities and their lower tuitions were available. A family friend recommended William & Mary. Williamsburg was 700 miles from Detroit, and the student and his parents knew little about the school. When the student asked his principal for advice, the educator looked into the distance and mulled over the question. Finally, he said, "I don't know much about William & Mary. But I think it's viewed favorably." The student applied with the blessing of his father and was admitted.

The Detroit student's dormitory—nicknamed the "Chicken Coop"—was a hastily built frame structure. During World War II, it served as the temporary barracks for the US Navy chaplains' school. The student's first night in the dormitory introduced him to one side of William & Mary life. He remembers that a classmate came back with "a few more beers in his stomach than he should have had." The Chicken Coop had a Coke machine on its first floor. The inebriated student took empty Coke bottles from the rack and set them up to form a rudimentary bowling alley. He then used another empty Coke bottle as a bowling ball and tried to knock over the ten upright bottles. Coke bottles rarely behave like bowling balls, so the drunk student's resourcefulness failed. He then loudly denounced the Coca- Cola Company and all of its descendants. In his anger he took a swing at the flimsy wall. Instead of punching a hole, however, his fist hit a stout two-by-four, circa 1942. The pain only caused him to increase his complaints in volume and creativity.

This experience with bottles and fisticuffs provided the freshman's introduction to the social side of William & Mary. Asked almost seventy years later whether these drunken incidents typified his years at William & Mary, he replied, "No, that night stands out. I never saw anything like it again. Other Virginia schools had drinking reputations, but William & Mary was not a party school. Yet, something like 48 percent of the males were in fraternities, so that did have an effect."

The freshman from Michigan spent his first two years taking required liberal-arts courses. He named professors in Spanish, chemistry, and history as his best teachers. As a junior he declared a major in economics. The early 1950s were the years of the Korean War. After graduation the student served on active duty as a naval officer. His active duty began just after the Korean Armistice was declared in July 1953.

The third alumnus was a native of Williamsburg. His father, a professor of economics and the first chairman of the Department of Business Administration at William & Mary, became dean of the faculty, and later president, of Wofford College. Because the alumnus had skipped a grade, his father wanted him to experience more education before entering college. For additional schooling, he sent his son to prestigious Deerfield Academy in Massachusetts. Most of his classmates at Deerfield planned to apply to Ivy League or Little Ivy League schools. Like Deerfield, those schools were all male. The son decided he wanted to attend a coed school. When the student returned to Williamsburg, he entered William & Mary as a member of a freshman class that consisted of 641 students and chose to live on campus. Although the student majored in chemistry, he remembers two professors of German as being "especially good." He graduated first in his class, earning all As except for one B—at that time, a rare occurrence. Following graduation from William & Mary, he took an MD degree from the Yale University School of Medicine. After an internship and residency in Boston, he went to the National Cancer Institute at the National Institutes of Health (NIH) and then had a hematology fellowship at the University of Utah. He returned to Yale as a faculty member and was one of the founders of the Section of Medical Oncology. His career was a combination of patient care, research, and teaching at Yale.

These three alumni attended a William & Mary that differed from the William & Mary of today. In 2021 William & Mary is a small university with master's and doctorate degree programs. But in the 1950s and for some years after, it was more like a small liberal-arts college. How did this Virginia college come to be?

Chartered in 1693 by King William III and Queen Mary of England as the second-oldest college (after Harvard) in America, it served initially as the tax-supported college of Virginia's established Church of England. It drew its support from the English monarchy, the Church of England, the colonial Virginia government, and the planter class. The original charter called for "one President, six Masters or Professors, and an hundred scholars more or less."[1] Its classrooms were full of sons of the Virginia gentry, and its charter emphasized good "arts and sciences." Among the early notable students were Thomas Jefferson, James Monroe, Benjamin Harrison, John Tyler, and Winfield Scott. All but one American university (University of Pennsylvania) founded in the colonial period were founded by Christian denominations. After the American colonies separated from England in 1776, William & Mary became an independent college loosely connected to the Episcopal Church. (Church of England parishes in the United States took the title "Episcopal" when they were no longer an official state church.) Eleven of its first twelve presidents were Anglican or Episcopal clergy. In 1781, during the Revolutionary War, the college closed due to the invasion of the British under Gen. Charles Cornwallis. It reopened the next year.

During the Civil War, most students left to enlist. In 1861, the faculty voted to close the college until 1865. In 1881, following the defeat of the Confederacy, the dearth of students and a lack of money caused the school to close again. Reopened in 1888 with a grant from the commonwealth of Virginia, William & Mary officially became a state-funded school in 1906. In its early decades under state control, it performed many of the functions of a teacher's college. In 1918, the first women students entered William & Mary. During the restoration of Colonial Williamsburg in the 1930s, the Main Building or Wren Building, the Brafferton former Indian school, and the William & Mary President's House were restored to their colonial appearance.

It was this colonial campus that welcomed the three alumni. They quickly found that William & Mary—like most colleges and universities in the 1950s—kept a firm hand on discipline. Classes met six days a week, and, as the vignette "The Early Morning Class" shows, faculty took attendance. Any student who cut class more than three times in a semester was subject to an automatic F. When students went home over Thanksgiving, they would receive an automatic F if they were not back on campus for their Monday morning class.

All students lived in dormitories, supervised by housemothers whose duties included enforcing "parietals" (strict rules that governed living on campus). Male undergraduates were not subject to curfews, but women had to be in their dorms by ten o'clock on weeknights and by midnight on weekends. Alcohol was forbidden in campus buildings. Unless women students were going to a physical education class, they could not wear shorts or slacks while on campus. The three students also quickly learned that an experienced housemother was difficult to deceive. Except for a tiny number of commuters, undergraduates could not have cars on campus in any year. To even ride in a car, women students—not male students—needed prior written permission from their parents.

The three 1950s alumni also remember that football played an active role in campus life. The university belonged to the Southern Athletic Conference, which included major athletic powers. After World War II, despite almost unanimous faculty opposition, the Board of Visitors (BOV) decided that a winning football program should become a campus-wide priority. The board earmarked significant funding for such a program. It also supported hiring a head coach who had gained national prominence for his record at the University of Tennessee. Not only was the new coach hired as the head coach, but he also became the head of the physical education department and the athletic department. This centering of power proved problematic.

The new funding included giving substantial financial aid for recruits who were high school football standouts. In fact, virtually all financial aid offered to students went to student athletes. Their academic records were of little concern to recruiters. After being accepted to William & Mary, most chose to major in physical education. As a censored series of editorials in the William & Mary *Alumni Gazette* declared in 1951, the administration had allowed football to become "powerfully absorbing" in practically all aspects of the college. To free up football players for practice in the afternoons, for example, the administration had added 8 a.m. classes to the curriculum.

Bulwarked by their recognized and well-paid coach, the postwar Indians, as the team was known then, became highly successful. More than twenty team members were drafted by the National Football League. In 1947, the team won the Southern Conference Championship. In 1948 it lost to Arkansas in the Dixie Bowl, but in the next year the team defeated Oklahoma A&M in the Delta Bowl.

But this emphasis on winning caused William & Mary to become a center of controversy. Victorious seasons depended on a steady stream of star recruits coming to the university each year to play. To ensure that they would come, William & Mary's athletic department began to alter the high school and college transcripts of football recruits, not only for admission but also for continued eligibility. The athletic director also arranged for credit to be added to transcripts for summer classes when student athletes were on campus for only a few days. In 1949 the college's registrar (a psychology professor and administrator viewed as "Mr. William & Mary") discovered this transcript altering; he investigated and reported his findings to the president. But William & Mary's Ivy League–trained president, who had a background on the faculties of Vanderbilt and Princeton, took no action against any member of the athletic department. The procedure for handling applications of the athletes, however, was revised.

In 1950, William & Mary joined the National Collegiate Athletic Association (NCAA), the organization that regulates competition and eligibility rules for intercollegiate sports in the United States. Many faculty were in favor of the membership, believing that the NCAA would force the college to revise its admission practices. That may have been true, but no significant change occurred. The emphasis on athletic prestige was apparently in Williamsburg to stay. In 1951, the dean of the college found that some football players continued to receive grades and credit for courses they had not taken. He investigated, and his conclusions ultimately led to the resignations of the head and assistant football coaches. Once they resigned, the president took no further action, saying he would temper justice with mercy.

The story was leaked to the press and widely publicized. It became known as "the Football Scandal of 1951"—a search term that garners plenty of results on the internet still today. The story became front-page news and brought undesired national notoriety to a historic school. The controversy caused a rift between the BOV and the faculty, who wanted control of all phases of intercollegiate athletics. William & Mary's president became the scapegoat. "He saw it coming," a leading faculty member told an interviewer. "He had his resignation all ready. He quickly accepted an offer to become director of the Huntington" (a prestigious research institution in California). When the president resigned, the BOV refused to allow any faculty participation in the search for his successor. The board quickly chose a former president's son, a Navy admiral with no academic background, as its new president. For the William & Mary football program, the 1950s were a time of secretive resolutions, pressure from the BOV on the president and faculty, meetings of influential alumni to discuss the program, and secretaries testifying about the altering of transcripts. The dean of the college resigned in protest after the new president was appointed.

A 2016 article about the scandal printed in the *Flat Hat*[2] student newspaper quotes the dean as saying in his letter of resignation: "The recent administration of our intercollegiate athletic program is dishonest, unethical, and seriously lacking in responsibility to the standards of William & Mary. I am puzzled at the realization that to resign is not to accomplish anything. It seems to constitute forfeiting the hope of so doing."

The football scandal wasn't the only impropriety that the three students experienced. In 1953—just before the three students graduated—an honor code violation involving a stolen exam resulted in the expulsion of thirty William & Mary students, eight of whom were starting football players. At that time, following basketball games in the Blow Gym, music was played to accompany the departure of the spectators. On the day the expelled students were to leave campus by midnight, one student recalled, the loudspeaker played "So Long, It's Been Good to Know You." Some of the departing audience, he recalled, grew pensive, since they had friends among the thirty.

During the following years at William & Mary, faculty members as well as students strongly debated the priorities of academics versus an all-encompassing commitment to athletics. That state of affairs has not been unusual in American colleges and universities that have put considerable resources into such programs and weathered occasional scandals. What is unusual is that William & Mary has faced the same challenges since the 1940s and overcome them. As late as the midsixties, the dean of the faculty told a new instructor to contact him immediately if any coaches asked for special favors for football players. Two coaches did, and the dean called them into his office. Unlike deans at most colleges and universities with prestigious athletics, he read them the riot act.

The three alumni from the 1950s all have fond memories of William & Mary. They agree that the education they received there has served them well in graduate school, careers, and life. The alumna says, "I didn't think much about William & Mary in the years immediately after graduation. There was so much else to do—marriage, children, master's degree in social work, job, etc. But in later years, I thought about that time in which I was ecstatically happy. We were blessed at William & Mary."

The Detroit alum retired in Williamsburg. He credits the professor who taught his required senior seminar in economics with giving him tools that proved valuable in his later graduate studies. He also tells the story of meeting his wife when she baked a raspberry pie for a party both attended. They began to date, and the pie became a Valentine's tradition until her death in 2018.

Reflecting on his choice of William & Mary, the Williamsburg native said, "The university was a wonderful academic experience because of the outstanding faculty. I made a large number of friends while there—many lifelong," he continued. "They came from organizations such as my dormitory, my fraternity, the student organization of my church, and the college choir. In fact, the best decision I ever made was to attend the university, for it was there in the choir I met my wife," he concluded. "She always claimed I walked her home from rehearsal after Wednesdays because that was the day that she got *Life* magazine in the mail, and I could read it."

2. Recollections of Choosing a College

As a high school senior in the 1990s, a young woman applied to seven undergraduate programs: those of Carleton College, Vanderbilt University, Amherst College, the University of Illinois, Princeton University, Smith College, and William & Mary. Their variety shows how unsure she was of what she wanted. She classified the seven schools as *northern, southern, small, huge, fancy, female,* and *William & Mary.* Others might have classified them with descriptions such as a *highly ranked midwestern college,* a *small southern university,* a *historic New England college,* a *huge state university,* a *fancy Ivy League school,* a *Seven Sister,* and William & Mary.

She found that choosing a college was fraught with weightiness in a way she did not fully expect. The choice represented the first time in her life that she was making a decision with truly life-altering consequences. That responsibility weighed heavily. For her, as for many high school seniors, even choosing which colleges to apply was a struggle. From her home in the suburbs of a major city, her parents had graciously transported her all over the eastern half of the country looking at colleges. If she had asked, she was confident they would have taken her around the western half of the nation as well. On these college trips, she viewed dozens of lovely quads, ivy-covered buildings, and dignified dining halls. After a while, she found that the colleges visited inevitably started to blend together. If she had been asked why she applied to seven colleges—not four, not nine—she would have been unable to explain.

To be sure, she was interested in science—and hence keen on the science buildings and courses at Smith. In addition, her older brother was a sophomore at Princeton. His being there clearly influenced that application. When she visited, Carleton struck her as "cozy," and Amherst seemed "worldly." Set in a vibrant and growing city, Vanderbilt caused her to reflect, "This looks like *fun*." As for the University of Illinois, half of her high school friends seemed to be headed there. Looking back, the alumna suspects that "a million intangibles" affected her perceptions of the seven colleges visited. The weather at the time, the quality of the tour guide, the "gut feeling" a place gave off—all of these things, plus others, she believes undoubtedly played a role.

In the end, she got into all seven of the colleges, and she chose William & Mary. In this case, the reason for the decision was clear. To her, the historic institution just felt like the right balance of many things: nerdy but not intimidatingly intellectual, and a nice medium size. As she notes, several of the seven schools were smaller than her high school. It also helped that Williamsburg had a comfortable climate. Plus, William & Mary had male students as well as female. The absence of males killed her Seven Sister application. The student's final choice came down to Princeton or William & Mary. When she chose William & Mary, she sensed that many of her teachers, counselors, and friends thought (in her words) "that I was a bit bonkers." But, as the student reflected, she realized that she would have chosen the historic Ivy League university primarily because it was what a friend called an "oooh school." She would not have selected it because it was *the* school for *her*. When she visited Princeton on her tour, she had what she called a "Stepford Wives" moment. The campus looked perfect. The students looked perfect.

But, it seemed to her, there was a certain falseness to it, as if everything were for show. To her, William & Mary came across as much more real, much more touchable. She experienced it as a warm beauty, as opposed to a cool, polished beauty. And that made all the difference.

William & Mary struck her as a sort of cocoon. At age seventeen, she needed such a cocoon. She was uneasy about leaving the familiarities of home and going to a school 900 miles away. She needed a place where almost every student lived on campus and where the social scene was heavily tilted toward board games and movie nights in dorm rooms. In addition, she recalled liking William & Mary's emphasis on undergraduate education. Both of her parents were teachers. Both were passionate about and committed to their profession. Hence, she knew what a difference good teachers can make. In college, she wanted to be taught by *the kind of teachers who really want to be in front of a classroom*. As her four undergraduate years progressed, she realized that she had been absolutely right to recognize that the emphasis on teaching would be a strength of William & Mary.

By the end of the four years, she realized that she had received a rich and substantive education as an undergraduate. She had been taught to think critically. She had been instructed in how to write with clarity and style. She had befriended her professors. And in her words, she had learned how to "make peace with being a decent student in a school of outstanding students." Finally, she observed, "I was able to do all of these things while seated in a storied building perched at the edge of Colonial Williamsburg."

Two decades after she graduated with a double major in chemistry and religious studies, the student wrote to one of her professors. She told him that ever since childhood she had gravitated toward locales that, for lack of a better term, had a bit of "ancient magic" to them. "I'm definitely into old beauty," she declared. "And William & Mary is steeped in old beauty."

3. Off to See the Wizard

After spending the junior and senior years of high school looking for the right college, a student from the Midwest had reduced her choices to Rhodes College, the University of Chicago, and William & Mary. "Rhodes was closer to home," she reflected in an interview. "It felt comfortable because it was small and I had friends there. My college-rating book ranked University of Chicago with the Ivies. And when I visited Chicago, I liked the beautiful campus. The downside was that it felt neither personal nor homey—and it was *expensive*."

The student visited William & Mary twice—the first during spring break in high school. She recalls, "My mother and I flew to Virginia, rented a car, and visited University of Virginia, William & Mary, and some schools in Washington, DC." Initially, William & Mary had not been on their list, but a family friend had recommended it. She and her mother made no special plans for their visit to Williamsburg, no fanfare or organized events. They simply took a guided tour of the campus. But they left Williamsburg impressed. "Although I had intended to apply to UVA," she remembers today, "I ended up liking William & Mary better."

The second visit to William & Mary took place in her senior year, after she had received acceptances from all three colleges. Each school had its own appeal. The competing choices, she recalls, "really started rolling around in my head. I was distraught about the whole thing." She found that William & Mary offered a Virtual Visit for students in April. Designed for admitted and prospective students, the Virtual Visit continues into the internet age the tradition of an academic open house. At William & Mary, representatives from every academic department— as well as from such offices as academic advising, student activities, financial aid, and residence life—log in to answer the students' questions. The student participated in two nights of the Virtual Visit, because she was "looking for answers or comradery or something," she remembers. "And that's where I first ran across the Wizard's chat room." After participating in the online forum, through which a professor at William & Mary answered prospective students' questions under the moniker "the Wizard," she decided that it would be helpful to have an in-person discussion with the Wizard about her college options.

If she could find a seat on a plane, her parents told her, she could fly out that very weekend and spend it at William & Mary. The parental offer had one proviso: that she come back from her weekend having decided which of the three colleges to attend. "To be sure," she later said, "flying to Williamsburg alone on such short notice was expensive. My parents, however, were eager to help me make a decision I wouldn't regret. In addition, I think they secretly approved of William & Mary for me and thought the visit might seal the deal."

The student did get an airline ticket for the next day. In Williamsburg she found a friend of a friend to stay with on campus. She ate with other students in the dining halls. "Of course," she reflects, "it was spring, the campus was gorgeous, trees were blooming, everything was turning green. But I hardly remember anything as distinctively as I remember my visit with the professor known as 'the Wizard.'"

Locating the Wizard, whose identity remained masked, presented a problem. She knew he was a William & Mary professor in one department or another. She started asking the students she met if they happened to know who the Wizard was. "Tracking the Wizard down was quite an adventure," she later recalled. "Finally, a student told me that he thought one of the professors teaching him that semester was the Wizard." And that identification turned out to be correct.

The professor named had an office in the historic Wren Building. "I wandered three stories of the building looking for his office," she said. "I am pretty sure that someone in the building directed me to the third floor. It felt like a different world up there—such an old building, so collegiate." And there, working on his computer in an office displaying his real name, was the Wizard. When she identified herself, the professor invited her into his office. They talked about college for about an hour. If she decided to attend William & Mary, the Wizard said he would be glad to take her as one of his dozen freshman-sophomore advisees.

How were the four years at William & Mary? Asked eight years after graduation, she answered, "Challenging—it really was a defining time in my life. Even though William & Mary was 'small,' it was much, much bigger than my one-hundred-person graduating class in high school. I was the school's newspaper editor—a big fish! But at William & Mary, I struggled to find my place at first ... I think that particular challenge did more to help build my character than I realized at the time. Things really started to fall into place my junior and senior years."

She continued, "I look back on that time very fondly. I really found myself in academics and research. I studied in Argentina, got funding from William & Mary to spend a summer working with a nonprofit in Mexico, and found mentors in history and Hispanic studies. I lived in the Spanish House on campus and had a close group of friends." Following graduation, she taught English in Spain for one year, then moved back to her home state for a year to work for an educational nonprofit. Then she moved to New York City to pursue a career in writing. To date, her work has appeared in publications ranging from the *New York Times* to the *Kansas City Star* to print and online literary journals. In its annual prose contest, the prestigious *Fugue Journal* named one of her short stories runner-up.

4. The Freshman Who Cut Classes

In the 1960s, a student who now describes his former self as a "brash" and "self-exalted freshman" entered William & Mary. Like most of the entering class, he had excelled in high school. At the time, William & Mary, like many colleges and universities, allowed a student to cut a class only three times in a semester. After three cuts, the student automatically failed the course. Most William & Mary faculty agreed with the policy, since the much-respected dean of the faculty endorsed this rule and wanted it enforced. "If students cut class in order to work in the library, then their cuts might be justifiable," he would say during the meetings of faculty that opened each academic year. "But they don't go to the library when they cut class."

The faculty who did not agree with the three-cut rule included the freshman English professor to whom the student was randomly assigned during registration. In his years at William & Mary, the professor had never reported a student to the dean's office because of excessive cuts. But he did not publicize his leniency. He believed that good teaching attracted students to a class. He also believed that students who frequently cut class would encounter serious difficulty passing his tests—because he tested not only assigned reading but also material covered in lectures. In the long run, he was confident that the students' absences would catch up with them and they would learn a valuable lesson.

The English class in which the freshman was enrolled met at eight o'clock in the morning on Tuesdays, Thursdays, and Saturdays. Six weeks into the fall semester, the over-confident student had already cut class three times. One Thursday, he missed his fourth class. During class that day, the professor announced to students that he was going out of town for the weekend and, as a result, was canceling their Saturday class. Later that afternoon, the delinquent student saw the professor walking on campus. Conscious that he had skipped class in the morning, he averted his gaze and walked quickly in the opposite direction. But the professor saw him, called to him, and said he wanted to talk.

The student expected he was going to be admonished for cutting class a fourth time. But no admonishments were forthcoming. Instead, the professor glanced around to make sure that no one on the brick walk was listening. Then in a low voice and conspiratorial tone, he suggested that the student would be wise to be especially well prepared for class on Saturday. Because, he strongly hinted, there might be a pop quiz Saturday on the material covered Thursday. The professor did not come right out and say there *would* be a test, but it was heavily implied. "And," said the professor, "I think too highly of you to let a quiz lower your final grade."

The necessity of privacy, the lowered voice, the conspiratorial tone— all served as a warning that there would be a surprise test Saturday morning. "I felt privileged to receive this insider information," the student wrote decades later. "It would give me a competitive advantage over the class. And it might also boost my grade-point average, which at William & Mary was turning out to be lower than I expected. I did not question why he had singled me out for the warning. I felt it was the kind of information I was entitled to." That night, the student read and reread the material he had missed in Thursday's class. By Friday evening, he felt thoroughly prepared for the pop quiz on Saturday. He celebrated by getting drunk.

When his alarm sounded at seven o'clock on Saturday morning, the freshman turned it off and went back to sleep. He woke up again at 7:35. Scrambling, he threw on clothes and rushed from his dormitory room. "I remember [him] waking in a panic and making a lot of noise as he left," his freshman roommate remembers today. "He woke me up on a Saturday morning—not good."

At the time, William & Mary had one off-campus dormitory several miles away that required a shuttle bus to get to campus. The student lived in that dormitory. When he got to its driveway, he found that the shuttle bus for eight o'clock classes had already left. In those years, sleepy Williamsburg had few cabs—and no Uber or Lyft. But in a frantic search, the student found a telephone number for one cab company. When the car arrived at the dorm, he exhorted the driver, "To the Wren Building, *and step on it!*" At 7:55 a.m., he arrived in front of the Wren Building. Built between 1695 and 1700, the Sir Christopher Wren Building is the oldest academic building not only at William & Mary but also in the United States. Restored by Colonial Williamsburg, it has the high ceilings and steep stairs of buildings of its era. Feeling the full effect of the alcohol he had consumed the previous night, the student raced up the steep stairs

and ran breathlessly into the classroom. It did not take him long to see that its desks, chairs, and lectern all were empty. A sign taped to the door read: "English 101 Canceled Today."

The student quickly surmised that the professor's warnings had been a setup. He had received utterly false information; he had been "had." How, the student pondered, should he—a cool guy—respond to this outrage? "I remember his coming back to the room ... alternately furious and amused as he told me about it," the roommate recalls.

"I remember the hour-long conversation discussing what to do. We discussed in delicious detail what an appropriate response would be to his professor. I also remember our concluding, with truly great glee, that his best revenge would be to refuse to give the professor the satisfaction of acknowledging the success of the trick."

So it remained for seven semesters. Before he graduated, the student and the professor were associated in three other courses. Although they often talked, neither referred to the freshman English course or to the class canceled that Saturday three years ago. Occasionally the professor speculated about that October morning. Had the student actually gone to the classroom? Had another member of the class informed him that the Saturday class had been canceled? Despite the forewarning that a pop quiz was likely, had the student just gone ahead and skipped anyway? The professor always ended up puzzled.

The story now shifts to the graduation of the student's class three years later. Until the 1970s, William & Mary held its commencement ceremonies on the spacious lawn of the Wren Building. When the ceremony was over, some faculty, students, and their families left for other destinations. Others remained on the lawn, chatting. Students would often seek out professors to say farewell, to thank them, or to introduce them to their parents. As the professor was leaving commencement, the student walked over to him and said, "I just wanted to tell you what happened that Saturday you canceled class."

The professor replied, "Now I would find *that* fascinating." And the student then told the professor about his frantic race to the Wren Building for class and his decision to say absolutely nothing about what had happened. The professor quickly realized that the joke had also been on him. From time to time during the past three years, he had puzzled over the possible sequence of events on that Saturday morning. The student knew what had happened, but his silence had kept the professor from knowing as well. The purpose of the hoax had been to teach a self-centered freshman that being irresponsible had consequences—but the faculty member had been outmaneuvered by the student's silence.

As the professor and student stood on the Wren lawn, rehashing the events of three years earlier, they laughed and laughed. Faculty, students, and families remaining on the lawn looked at them and wondered, "What in the world could possibly be so funny?"

5. A Masterpiece of Humor, Scorn, and Invective

During a mid-1960s academic year, two freshmen who were close friends signed up to take William & Mary's four-credit, full-year introductory course in geology. Completing the course required three hours of lectures and three hours of lab exercises weekly. It would satisfy their freshman science requirement. The introductory classes for chemistry, physics, and biology would also satisfy that requirement, but the two students had heard what they described as "nightmare stories" about the difficulty of those courses.

Initially, one of the two students thought he would have an easy time in the geology course. Geology is the study of the earth. As a child he had liked rocks, collected them, and later even earned a Boy Scout merit badge in geology. And on some campuses, the introductory geology course was easy. At those schools the course was known as "Rocks for Jocks." The freshman was not above cunning calculation. Perhaps, he thought, William & Mary's geology department also taught its own version of "Rocks for Jocks." But he could not have been more mistaken. As it turned out, William & Mary's introductory course was no walk in the park. Four faculty then formed William & Mary's Department of Geology. Although they had a reputation for being good teachers, some students disliked the professor who taught the introductory course. Now in his early thirties, this professor held three degrees from an Ivy League university. He was known for high standards. The lecture portion of the introductory geology course met in a large auditorium. The labs for the course were much smaller. The classes required field trips. One trip, one of the freshmen remembers, was to the golf course of the Williamsburg Inn. There, he recalls, the students "pecked around in a shelf of exposed fossils, shells, and calcified marine life." The second semester was not quite over when the professor assigned the class a topographical map project. In the description of the student, it was a "beast of an assignment." In the mid-1960s, William & Mary's campus ended with the newly constructed Yates Hall. Beyond Yates, the campus consisted of woods, brambles, a gorge, and a stream. Scattered about in this semiwilderness were stakes embedded in the ground. They were marked with scientific symbols and elevation markers. Every year the professor required his introductory students not only to find these stakes but also to draw a topographical map based on the information they found. In theory, the more markers students found, the more accurate their map and its indications of metallic deposits and elevations.

The night before the project was due, the male freshman stayed up all night to complete it. As the sun was rising, he went over to help his friend with her map. He found her "frantic, in tears" because of the difficulty of finishing the project. "As we worked," he remembers, "I kept nodding off and telling her that I had to go back to my dorm and get some sleep, but she kept saying, 'But you *promised*, you *promised*.'" The two freshmen kept working on her map until they finished it. Later that day, they submitted their projects in class.

Like many students in the class, the two freshmen found the assignment of the topographical map unreasonable. "Sadistic in its difficulty," the male student later described the project. For a professor to expect that level of work from freshmen, he thought, was unrealistic. Today, fifty years later, that critical freshman is now himself an emeritus professor of history. In retrospect, he guesses the topographical map was the kind of project the geology professor himself had done as a student at Yale. But for most freshmen, the assignment simply seemed a bridge too far. The professor emeritus remembers the warning his dissertation advisor in history at Yale later gave to him: "Be sure not to demand as much from your future undergraduate students as I have demanded of you as a graduate student."

The map proved such an ordeal that it prompted the male freshman, with the help of his friend, to write what he today calls a "sarcastic screed about our dreaded, hated professor." Written secretly in the days following the submittal of the project, the diatribe contained—in its author's words—"ridicule, cynicism, juvenile attempts at wit, and the usual undergraduate bombast." At the time the two freshmen viewed their diatribe as "a masterpiece of humor, scorn, and invective." They kept adding to it until it became what they thought was a magnum opus. The male student typed the final version on his portable Royal typewriter. At a late hour the next night, the two freshmen took their letter over to the geology department. Finding, as they expected, the doors closed but unlocked, the lights off, and no one in the halls or offices, they posted the missive on the department bulletin board. Then they returned to the dormitories without being discovered.

The student remembers the several weeks remaining in the semester as "excruciating." The geology professor had obviously received the letter. He was plainly upset, and his displeasure showed in class. He did not go on a rampage, but he did ask many students and colleagues if they knew who had written the letter. But no one, other than

the two authors, knew the answer. Throughout those final weeks of the academic year, the freshmen were terrified that their authorship would be discovered. They agreed to keep the information from even their closest friends. Half a century later, the secret essentially holds.

As the four years of undergraduate education went on, the two students gradually began to see the letter as an embarrassment. They came to view it as a "stupid thing," something that was not worth the risks they had taken. "But oh," the alumnus remembers today, "did writing that letter *feel good* at the time."

After decades of college teaching, the author had gained a different perspective on the geology professor and the kind of obstacles he had routinely faced. "Overworked and underpaid, our professor was teaching introductory courses to students who weren't going to major in geology or in any other science. That couldn't have been enjoyable," he notes. "But he didn't teach 'Rocks for Jocks.' Instead, he had high expectations for William & Mary students. In other words, he brought *rigor* to the classroom. There was probably little difference between the standards imposed in this course compared to those imposed at his Ivy League alma mater. He was far from unreasonable. Being held to high standards was good for us. Fifty years later, I'm not proud of the letter we wrote."

6. All That Jazz

As a high school student, he had been named to the Minnesota's All-State Jazz Ensemble twice. As a high school senior, he had been named "Best Improviser" in Minnesota. At the time, he seriously considered applying to a conservatory of music and following a musical career. In the end, he decided to apply only to liberal-arts programs. He had excelled in history in high school. The subject interested him more than playing jazz.

When he arrived at William & Mary, he felt far from home—but that was exactly what he had wanted when he applied to schools far from home. There were clear educational advantages to continuing studies at a distance from the Twin Cities. For four years—by plane, train, car, and bus—he traveled to and from college through states he had never visited. Riding on some occasions with another William & Mary undergraduate who lived in the Twin Cities, he traveled through Illinois, Indiana, Ohio, West Virginia, and Maryland to get back to college. If he took what he viewed as the southern route to Virginia, he drove through Wisconsin, Illinois, Indiana, Kentucky, and West Virginia.

In Williamsburg he shared dormitories with students from widely diverse hometowns in America. By literally expanding his horizons and attending college far from Minnesota, he felt that he learned as much outside class as he did in it. In addition, just being a Minnesotan in Virginia proved educational. "Minnesota?" a Richmond native asked during freshman orientation. "Why, Minnesota wasn't even a *state* when the Civil War happened." The

Minnesotan freshman responded that Minnesota became a state in 1858. And, he continued, the First Minnesota Infantry Regiment saved the Union cause at Gettysburg. The Minnesotans charged into a full brigade of Confederate soldiers on Cemetery Ridge and suffered the worst one-day casualty rate (82 percent) of any infantry regiment in the Civil War. That information, he remembered, seemed "to shut my new friend up."

During his time at William & Mary, the student played in the William & Mary Jazz Ensemble and in a small-group jazz combo formed with friends. "It is a great way to meet people," he said, "and it continued to feed my passion for jazz." He performed at Phi Beta Kappa Hall, at the Williamsburg Inn in the restored area of Colonial Williamsburg, in bars, at receptions, and in a student-run coffee shop where the more free-spirited undergraduates hung out. The Minnesotan spent the most time, however, with his major of history. After graduating with highest honors, he took the master of arts and doctorate degrees in Western history. Currently the chair of the Department of History at Augsburg University in Minneapolis, he has gained a reputation for the high quality of his publications and the excellence of his classroom teaching.

High school seniors bolster their applications to college by listing special skills. Getting admitted to William & Mary from a Plains state was not easy. The student's application to colleges included the academic awards he had won in history. But probably few applications to William & Mary or to any college that year included an All-State Award for jazz.

During the student's senior year in college, one of his professors learned of his awards in jazz. "All-State in jazz?" he declared. "That's splendid. It will help with your graduate applications."

"Yes, but *look*," the Minnesota senior replied. "Honestly, being named to the All-State Jazz Band in Minnesota isn't that hard.

States like Texas, California, Illinois, New York—they have magnet high schools specializing in music. Those high schools produce jazz musicians and even bands who are known the world over. In Minnesota, we had little of that—but we had *fun*."

7. The Three-Page Two-Page Paper

When literary critic Arthur Quiller-Couch coined the term "murder your darlings," it was his metaphorical way of saying that writers are sometimes forced to cut treasured words from their work. American novelist William Faulkner liked the phrase but incorrectly remembered it as "kill all your darlings." Faulkner's version became common usage. At William & Mary, faculty who taught Freshman English often used the phrase to explain page limitations to their classes: "Two pages—not three. Not two pages with small type and crimped margins. Just submit papers of no more than two pages in length. All class members have the same space in which to express their ideas. You can do it. Sometimes, you know, we just have to 'kill our darlings.'"

Institutions of higher education have traditionally sought to teach their students to write clearly and well. For many decades, colleges and universities did that by requiring students to take courses in rhetoric. Defined as "the study and uses of written, spoken, and visual language," rhetoric courses were part of William & Mary's curriculum as far back as colonial times. By the 1960s, William & Mary's original rhetoric course had developed into a two-semester course known as "Freshman English" or "Writing." During each semester, students submitted eight two-page papers. Professors wrote comments on the papers, added a grade, and returned them as quickly as possible. As often as possible, professors would meet individually in their offices with students to discuss a paper. Satisfactory completion of these two semesters of writing was essential for a student to achieve sophomore status.

Every semester faculty would explain to the freshmen why these papers required page limitations. The hours simply were not there, they would point out, for students to write eight long papers in one semester. And for professors with heavy teaching loads, the hours also were not there to read and grade eight long papers from every student in their class of freshmen. Moreover, professors noted, students would often find themselves in situations after college where they needed to express ideas concisely. By learning in college how to "kill their darlings," students would develop the ability to avoid rambling repetition and sloppiness. In sum, learning how to express ideas concisely would serve the students well throughout college and life. Few students failed to understand the purpose of these instructions. Many of the students had written two-page papers ever since in high school.

One member of the freshman English faculty came to William & Mary with degrees from two prestigious universities. As a student at those schools, she had observed the high standards the two universities required in their freshman English courses. In Williamsburg, she imposed the identical standards on her students. She was a rigorous and scrupulous grader of writing. She did not reward sloppy work. Freshmen who had received As in writing throughout high school often received lower grades in her courses. Inevitably some complained about her grading. But after graduation—and, in fact, often before it—most students who had taken her freshman English courses recognized that she had done a remarkable job. They realized that they had emerged from her classes as much better writers than they had been when they entered college. In addition, they appreciated that they wrote better than many of the people with whom they worked.

One fall semester, the registration process assigned the valedictorian of an out-of-state high school to the professor's freshman English class. After two weeks in the course, the student submitted her first paper. It was more than a page too long. In her written comments, the professor reminded the student that the rules of the Department of English, the course syllabus distributed to all students, and her directions to the class declared that papers should be no longer than two pages. No other student in the nineteen-member class, she pointed out, had exceeded that limit.

The student undoubtedly read the comments on her paper. But when she submitted her second paper, it almost filled a third page. Again, it was the only paper submitted in the class that went beyond the two pages. After that class, the professor asked the student to stay to talk. In the conversation, she reminded the freshman that the rules of the

Department of English, the syllabus for the course, and the directions given numerous times in class specified that no paper should exceed two pages. She again pointed out that all other students in the class had met that requirement.

When the student turned in her next paper, however, it too continued into a third page. This time the professor wearily counted the words—a tedious task. Normally, the word total for a two-page paper

would approximate five hundred words. This paper was close to *seven* hundred words. Shaking her head, the professor marked the paper with an F and added a note about the two-page limit. When the papers were returned during the next class, the student looked at her grade, stood up, and walked out of the classroom.

What happened next was unusual for William & Mary's campus. The episode of "the three-page paper" became a cause célèbre. The student immediately called her parents. She also went to the student newspaper, the *Flat Hat,* and told them of the F. In its next issue, the paper ran an editorial criticizing "conformists" in the English department. In the meantime, the student's parents telephoned the president of William & Mary. The president spoke to the dean of the faculty. The dean of the faculty contacted the chair of the Department of English. The director of freshman English then called the professor in for a meeting.

"Look," the professor said in the meeting. "This student has probably been ignoring rules since kindergarten. She plainly thinks that directions are for others—she is *above* them. She feels *entitled*—and I don't like that. And if she gets her way on these papers, she receives an unfair advantage over other students. She can stretch out her arguments; she can take more space to develop her ideas. I've read all of her papers. They aren't *better* than those written by some other members of the class—they're just *longer*. And I can guarantee that she's done this kind of thing before."

Throughout the several weeks the controversy lasted, the professor remained impenitent. On the door of her office, she hung a big sign that read: "I am the professor who failed the three-page two-page paper." Her position was strengthened when the *Flat Hat* learned that the majority of the class supported the professor's decision. They then ran a new editorial modifying their criticism. For the rest of the semester, the student submitted papers that conformed to the two-page limit. She received a final grade of B, which in the 1960s was still viewed as a good grade. The student chose English as her academic major, but for the rest of her days at William & Mary, she avoided all contact—even eye contact—with the professor. She became known among other faculty in the department as a student to be treated with kid gloves.

Decades later, a colleague who had been on the faculty during the controversy asked the professor whether she would handle the incident of "the three-page paper" differently. Surprisingly, the professor answered, "Heavens, yes. I overreacted." When the colleague asked what she would do differently, the professor replied, "I would simply return the papers without a grade until she submitted one of correct length."

"But what if she kept on acting as if the rules didn't apply to her?"

"Then I'd make an appointment and take her to meet with the dean of the faculty," said the professor.

"You wouldn't give her an F?"

"No, not unless the dean recommended it. The ungraded papers piling up on her desk would be penalty enough."

"A lot of years have passed since that controversy. I wonder if she's still furious about the F you gave her on that paper."

"No, I don't think so."

"You don't? Why not?"

"Because we're both older."

8. A Different Approach to Grading

At an end-of-the-semester faculty gathering, a professor from one of William & Mary's departments approached a professor from another department. "Do you still teach those courses," she asked, "in which you send students out to do projects?"

"Yeah, I still teach them."

"Well, maybe you can help me. I used teams this year in my introductory course—first time. And they didn't work out."

"What was the problem?"

"Well, I assigned three students to each team. And I received complaints from several teams that one of their members was leaving the work for the others to do."

"Not pulling their weight?"

"Exactly. And on one team, a male member *really* sat on his hands. The other members of his team reported that he didn't come to their planning meetings. He didn't show up for one of their trips. In fact, he didn't even contribute to their project paper."

The other professor nodded her head. "Now that I remember it, when I began using teams, I had the same problem," she said. "But then I began to require every team to add an honor statement to their semester paper. All members signed the statement. It indicated who did what on the project. After I added that requirement, the problems started to disappear. I still require those statements."

"You know," replied the other professor, "I'm going to try something like that—or else simply stop assigning projects. The last thing I need in my life right now is another team complaining about freeloaders."

"So what grade did you give to the team member who *was* a freeloader?"

The other professor grimaced, and then spoke in rueful terms. "Well, I had ... I had to give him a B."

9. The Case of the Purloined Exams

In the 1970s, a popular professor who handled one of the largest introductory courses on campus was alerted to disturbing news. Students in his course had been obtaining copies of his hourly tests before they were given. Now, he was told, these students planned to steal a copy of the final examination. Three fifty-minute tests, plus a three-hour final exam, determined a student's semester grade in that course. The professor learned the same group had, in one way or another over the years, obtained keys to various offices on the campus. A member of the group whom the professor sardonically called the "Keeper of the Keys" would enter a professor's office late on the night before a test or exam. After taking one copy of the exam from the stack in the file cabinet, he would carry that copy back to share and discuss with the group. The pile of two-hundred-plus exams was sufficiently large that one copy was not missed.

Previously, the professor had been unaware that students were stealing his tests. Now that he had been alerted, he pondered what to do. After substantial reflection, the professor decided to take no action—or, rather, what *appeared* to be no action. He wrote a careful and thorough final exam. He ran off copies. After counting the total, he put the copies of the exam in the usual place in his file cabinet in his office.

But then the professor wrote a *second* final exam that contained entirely *different* questions. He stored this test in his car. When the professor arrived at his office on the morning of the exam, he took the first exams out of the file cabinet and counted them. As he expected, one was missing. He went to his car, retrieved the second final exam, and carried it into the large lecture hall.

When he distributed the exam, most students settled down to answer its questions. But the professor observed "a degree of semi-panic among certain areas of the class." Some students urgently shuffled through the pages of the exam looking for the questions they had found on the exam they had stolen. Others stood up, looked around for their buddies, and exchanged looks—in the professor's description—of "confusion, alarm, and puzzlement."

The result? In the words of the professor, "Perhaps fifteen or twenty students who up to this point had been 'earning' passing grades [brought] their semester averages down substantially. A few still passed the course, but many now failed it."

To make up for failing the course and to remain eligible in the fall, some of the students involved went to summer school. That year the professor also taught in the summer session. "Some of these students and I passed each other on campus every day of summer school," he later recalled. "I greeted each in passing with a friendly hello, whether the student averted his eyes or glowered ... so the last laugh was mine. Justice ultimately prevailed, although a bitter aftertaste remained."

Several years later, when the professor was teaching the same course from a new office, he could not find his grade book late in the semester. "Perhaps it had been thrown out, maybe left somewhere, or just 'lost,'" he later reflected. No other record of the three hourly tests the class had taken existed outside of that grade book. After reflection, the professor made his students an offer. Students could erase their grade record and use in its place *only* their grade on the three-hour final examination. Alternately, not only could they give him a note stating their three previous test scores, but they could also take the final exam. The professor would enter the three scores in a new grade book, add in the grade scored on the final exam, and calculate their semester grade. His assumption was that students who had been doing poorly in the course would choose the first option. He also assumed that those who had been doing well in the class would select the second option. To the professor's surprise, almost all of the students who had been doing poorly chose the second option. They reported hourly test grades—such as 43 percent, 57 percent, 38 percent, etc.—that would receive a failing grade. The professor was impressed. "How honest of them!" he thought.

This display of personal integrity, even when a more favorable option was offered, more than erased the professor's disappointment with the stolen-exam experience of a few years earlier. Over the years until retirement, he saw this second course as the truer expression of the essential honesty of the students he taught at William & Mary, later writing to another faculty member, "Redemption indeed, sweet to the taste."

10. The General and the Final Examination

The William & Mary professor was in his office when the phone rang. The semester was over. He had finished grading the examinations and semester papers of the students enrolled in his three courses.

Now he was clearing the clutter of the examination period from his desk. He was writing letters to students—congratulatory ones to those who had done well in his courses, supportive ones to those who had not. In offices all around him, his colleagues were doing much the same thing.

The professor picked up the phone on the third ring, and the caller identified himself as an Army major general. "I'm calling you," he declared, "from my office. In the Pentagon." If you taught at an institution of higher education located only 150 miles from the nation's capital, the professor reflected, you often taught children of notable figures. He had, in fact, taught the daughter of the chairman of the Joint Chiefs of Staff—and her father outranked this caller. He had also taught the children of multiple governors, senators, and congressmen.

"I'm the father of _____," the general said, naming a student whom the professor had failed and written a supportive letter. "And I intend to come down to Williamsburg to talk with you about my son's grade." His tone was that of a drillmaster.

"Yes, I could do that," said the professor. Faculty members were rarely wise to avoid meeting with irate parents.

"What time do you start work?" barked the general. The professor replied, "Between, uh, 8 and 9 a.m." He fudged a little because the Army was on a different timetable from the university. When the semester was over, he tended to arrive at his office closer to 9:30 or 10:00. He enjoyed lingering over the *New York Times* at his breakfast table.

The general ended the conversation. "Then I'll see you then at 0800 tomorrow. I have your office address. Good day."

After hanging up the phone, the professor sat thinking. He had served in the Army, and he recognized the tone of command. It was clear that he was about to get "dressed down." He had last heard that tone several decades earlier during a barrack inspection. The professor decided that he would be unwise to meet alone with the general. After reflecting on his options, he telephoned the associate dean of the faculty. As luck would have it, the associate dean was in his office and not in one of his many meetings. The professor related the situation to him.

"I'll be glad to sit in with you," said the dean. "0800—I guess that means 8 a.m., huh? But first, can you tell me something about how this guy's son performed in your class?"

The professor explained it in some detail, although there wasn't much to explain. The boy was simply unprepared. His midsemester exam and blue book had made it clear he had read few of the assignments; his paper was a brief, scanty piece of research handed in late. The professor and the dean decided to meet in the lobby of the professor's office building at 7:50 the next morning.

In the morning, the professor walked to his office. The dean arrived at about the same time. When the two took the elevator to the third floor, an older man—lean, weathered, dressed in civilian clothes, but in bearing and haircut clearly military—was standing by the door. The general introduced himself.

"My son tells me that his failing grade in your course was unfair," he said after taking a chair in the office. "He tells me that he was thoroughly prepared for the final examination. My son also says you ask irrelevant questions on your exams. And further, I should inform you, Professor, that my son also says that you take pleasure in failing students in your classes—that you actually *like* giving Fs—*and* that everybody knows it."

The professor's three-hour final examination had consisted of an objective, short-answer section (counting 25 percent of the exam grade) and three essays (counting 75 percent of the grade). When grading, the professor read each student's essays twice, and additional times if a grade was not obvious at that point. It was also his practice to grade the objective sections of exams before the essays. He numbered one side of a yellow legal pad vertically from twenty-five to twelve and one-half in increments of one-half. On the reverse side, the numbers continued from twelve down to zero. The numbers stretched over forty-nine lines and two sides of the yellow pad. As he graded and totaled his students' scores, the professor entered their last names on the appropriate lines.

He had long used this system. It alerted him to curve exams if the objective section had unintentionally proved too difficult. It also tended to identify the most prepared and least prepared students in the course.

He began grading essays by reading those of the students who had scored highest on the objective section. Sometimes there was no correlation between how a student performed on the objective section and the essay, but usually there was. Over the years he had received few complaints about grades. He invariably received high ratings in that category on student evaluations.

"Maybe I can best explain to you, sir," began the professor, "what your son's performance on the exam was by showing you this list."

GLIMPSES OF A PUBLIC IVY

He had decided to speak deferentially, as if he were still a grunt in the Army. He showed the general the yellow legal pad and explained what its numbers meant. "Let me see that list," the general said, taking the yellow pad firmly out of the professor's hands. The general scrutinized the list and then said, "Why, *there it is. There's* the answer. An error in your grading right from the beginning.

My son's name is not even *on* this list."

"Oh yes, sir," replied the professor. "It is. He's on the second page."

The general turned the pad over. And there, separated by nine lines from the nearest student, was the name of the general's son. He had scored eleven out of a possible twenty-five points on the objective section. The median of the class had been twenty-one points. The name of the general's son was all alone at the bottom of the class.

When the professor handed the student's exam to the general, he said, "Your son's essays were the same quality as his objective section, sir. One of his essays was only two paragraphs long."

Almost instantaneously, the atmosphere in the office changed. The general thumbed through the brief exam (which was the shortest in the class), took one last look at the yellow legal pad, and then said, in a tone of regret, "I owe you two men an apology. My wife told me to do this. I didn't want to drive down here from Washington this morning. My son has *never* lived up to his potential. He's just a goof-off. He expects someone else to take care of his problems. I was amazed when he was admitted to William & Mary."

The professor and the dean were parents too. They tried to add a positive note. They talked about how students often mature in college. The professor told the general that he himself had been a "world-class goof-off" until he experienced two years of military service in an infantry division.

"Draftee?" asked the general, perking up. "Yes, sir."

"What division?" the general asked. "Twenty-fifth."

"Good outfit," the general declared. "Guadalcanal, Pusan Perimeter, Japan—but you were probably stationed at Schofield Barracks, eh?"

"Yes, sir."

By the time the general left the office ten minutes later, all animosity had disappeared. Before he left, he invited the associate dean and the professor to his home. "The next time you're in northern Virginia, do call," he said. "I'll have you over for dinner. The houses they give us generals at Fort Myer on Generals' Row are something to behold." After the general left, the associate dean commented,

"You know, he's actually a nice guy."

"I thought so too," responded the professor.

Neither the professor nor the associate dean ever found it possible to accept the general's invitiation to dinner. But the associate dean was so taken with the episode that he spoke of it often. He told others, "I've dined out on that story for years."

11. Saved by Works

As the semester progressed at William & Mary, it became clear that the professor who taught the Protestant and Catholic Reformations and the top student in the class disagreed about central issues. A better way to explain their differences might be to say that the professor favored Martin Luther while the student favored Pope Leo X. Their disagreement prompted many useful intellectual discussions in class. On matters where the student held traditionalist or conservative views, the professor tended to be moderate. In matters of church doctrine and worship, the student believed in the correctness of medieval practices, while the professor was suspicious of them. Where most class members believed that the Reformation had brought distinct benefits to Western society, the traditionalist student felt the opposite.

A central question of the Reformation focused on whether humans are "saved" by their faith or by their works. At one class meeting, the professor lectured on the assertion of Martin Luther, John Calvin, and other sixteenth-century reformers that works done on earth and viewed as "good" are in reality tainted by such human defects as pride, egotism, or dishonesty. To the Protestant reformers, God does not see marred actions as good works. Luther, Calvin, and other Protestant leaders therefore believed that salvation must come from faith in Jesus Christ rather than from performing so-called good works. In the lecture on the Reformation one morning, the professor raised the question of whether this central claim of Protestant Christianity could be dead wrong. "Perhaps," he declared, "people should dismiss it outright. After all, to say that no human acts please the Judeo-Christian God is a *radical* assumption." The professor then reflected, "But, you know, if I were to look back with ruthless honesty at my own life, I would probably see that I've never done one single work *free* of such flaws."

Until this point, the professor was lecturing from notes.

His statement about looking back on his life was in his notes. But after he made that assertion, an irresistible thought suddenly struck him. He ad-libbed, "No, that's inaccurate. Come to think of it, I definitely *have*

done one pure work in my life. In 1968 I voted for Hubert Humphrey for president."

Hearing the comment, the traditionalist student—whom the class knew was very much a Republican—sat bolt upright. His expression became one of fury and indignation. He called out loudly to the professor, "Then, you had better hope that you are justified by faith and not by works."

This instance of lèse-majesté was the first such episode any of these students had witnessed in a class. It was also the first time that the professor had experienced such open hostility in the classroom. That a student would show such blatant disrespect to a professor, especially over a mere joke, shocked the class. And then the stunned students saw the professor. He was convulsed with laughter. He was laughing so hard that he was holding on to the podium to keep from collapsing to the floor. With the tension lifted, the class broke out into high hilarity. For most, this was the funniest episode they had witnessed in any of their classes.

The traditionalist student, however, did not share in the merriment. He was livid and continued to glare at the professor. The hilarity of the other students continued for several minutes—a long time in a classroom. Finally, the professor began to lecture again but found that he could not keep from occasionally laughing.

Today, the professor and the student (now himself a church historian at a theological seminary) are still in touch. The professor, now retired, continues to view the student's response to his ad-lib about Hubert Humphrey as the funniest event that occurred in any of the classes he taught. In the intervening years, he had changed to the extent that he no longer brought political ideology into the classroom. He also believes that he should not have told the partisan joke in the classroom. But he continues to remember with delight the rowdy disorder it caused.

Three versions of this incident have developed among William & Mary alumni over the decades. Today, some alumni of the course remember that their classmate proclaimed: "*Yes, and you will be judged for that too.*" They, of course, could be wrong.

The "Green Machines" transported students around campus and on field trips. *Photo courtesy of University Archives, Special Collections Research Center, William & Mary Libraries*

Other alumni remember their classmate's wording exactly as the professor does: "*Then, you had better hope that you are justified by faith and not by works.*" They, of course, could also be wrong.

Today the student himself remembers that he calmly responded: "*I am very glad that you are justified by faith.*" But he, like Martin Luther or Pope Leo X, or both, could always be wrong.

12. The Green Machine

One afternoon in the 1980s, some thirty dancers from the Orchesis Modern Dance Company left the dance studio of the Adair Gymnasium. Two members of the dance faculty, and the friend of one, accompanied them. The group was going to see the famous Martha Graham Dance Company perform at the Kennedy Center in Washington, DC. A part of William & Mary since 1941, Orchesis encourages undergraduates not only to develop their technical and performance skills, but also to participate in the art of choreography.

For transportation to Washington, the group traveled on what was known as "the Green Machine." Described with a smile as "really an institution" by the longtime vice president of student affairs, that was the generic term used for the buses that ran on routes from one end to the other on William & Mary's campus. Somewhat inaccurately also called "JBT" buses, they were the mode of transportation used by students who lived several miles away in temporary dormitories on James Blair Terrace.

The white-roofed buses were painted in green, with lettering in gold or yellow—William & Mary's colors. "Green Machines were basically school buses," a William & Mary graduate and staff member recalls. "No reclining seats, no seatbelts. To ride in one was like being back in grade school. I don't remember them as being tremendously dilapidated, but some had been in use for many years." After reflection, the alumnus added, "You felt sorry for anyone you saw regularly riding the Green Machine to the dorms at James Blair Terrace. Because if you lived at JBT, you were basically in Siberia."

Occasionally other student groups used Green Machines for trips. On one such trip back from Charlottesville, the bus—which carried the soccer team—lost its brakes. After standing on the brake pedal to no avail, the driver down-shifted gears and got the team safely off the interstate. They waited in a service station for a replacement bus to arrive from Williamsburg. "Green Machines," in the description of an alumnus, "were the bottom line of public transportation."

The plans for the dance company's trip to Washington almost changed when the driver scheduled for the group turned up sick. At the last minute, another William & Mary driver declared that he thought he knew how to get to the Kennedy Center and could drive them. The faculty in charge had allotted four hours to reach Washington, DC, but the discussion about a driver had consumed time. In addition, Green Machines had speed limiters—or governors—on their motors. This kept them from traveling as fast as most vehicles on the highway. Hence, on highways they poked along in the right-hand lane.

Nevertheless, the bus had navigated rush hour in Richmond and was approaching Washington when—somewhere near the Pentagon—the substitute driver abruptly pulled off to the side of I-95. In a forlorn voice, he confessed, "I'm lost." A collective gasp, followed by an intense discussion, issued from the passengers. The students hadanticipated this trip for months. Finally, after some minutes, a passenger broke in to say that he was "pretty sure" that he could direct the driver to the Kennedy Center. This discussion took time. The bus arrived at the doors of the Kennedy Center just as the lights were dimming and the curtain was about to rise. The members of the William & Mary group moved into the theater as quietly as they could. But thirty-three people cannot take seats in the second row of a theater just as the performance is beginning without creating a stir. For at least a minute, the William & Mary contingent was the center of attention for virtually everyone in the audience. Ushers and audience members were clearly annoyed, since arriving late at the theater—especially in a large group—is bad manners.

The group found the dance company's performance superb—and well worth the round trip from Williamsburg. Afterward, most of the students and faculty went directly back to the bus, but several students went backstage to secure Martha Graham's autograph. In the parking lot, the Green Machine stood in stark contrast to the chartered buses and glistening conveyances used by other audience members to get to the performance. To their dismay, the students saw that audience members filing into the parking lot were pointing to the Green Machine and laughing. For the students, there was no hiding. The bus stood out like a proverbial sore thumb. And the bright yellow letters on its sides definitively identified it as the property of William & Mary.

In daily life, the students generally found the Green Machines funny. In the presence of Washington patrons of culture, they felt embarrassed. The rattletrap bus seemed poor public relations for William & Mary—and for that matter, for the seriousness of their studies. Some of the dancers wondered if the Green Machine would tarnish William & Mary's reputation in the Washington area. As soon as the autograph seekers returned to the bus with Martha Graham's signature, the bus fled the Kennedy Center. Four hours later, an hour and a half longer than it would take any other vehicle, it arrived back at William & Mary's campus.

Students lost their campus belongings when Jefferson Hall burned. *Photo courtesy of University Archives, Special Collections Research Center, William & Mary Libraries*

The retired William & Mary soccer coach estimates that during his years of coaching, Green Machines were used about 90 percent of the time around campus. He estimates that they were used about 10 percent of the time for sporting or other events—such as this memorable trip to the Kennedy Center. As the years went on, the coach reports, vans and charter buses gradually replaced Green Machines. Ultimately William & Mary merged its bus system with the local transit authority, and the tradition of the Green Machines ended. But in their heyday, they made life interesting.

13. When Jefferson Hall Burned

The wife of a longtime faculty member went for her usual walk after her husband left for his 8 a.m. class. She followed one of her customary routes: down Pollard Park, through Chandler Court, past nationally known librarian Earl Gregg Swem's imposing home, and then over to Jamestown Road. From there, she would walk past the Campus Center and the Williamsburg Drug Store and into Colonial Williamsburg. She loved that walk.

But when she reached the Swem house this January morning in 1983, she saw fire engines, police cars, coils of fire hose, and clusters of people talking. She looked for the cause of the commotion. Jefferson Hall, a three-story dormitory that had been completely renovated one semester earlier, was burning. She stood looking at the destruction. The building's roof had collapsed. Its entire west wing was destroyed. Dark smoke rose from its ruins. Now devoid of windows and doors, the dormitory's rooms were exposed to the elements and covered with soot.

From bystanders, the faculty spouse learned what had happened. Shortly after one o'clock in the morning, the residents of Jefferson Hall had experienced what they thought was a fire drill. Since the hour was late and the temperature freezing, the 183 students—all second-semester freshmen, except for the resident advisors—initially participated with reluctance and irritability. But it was no drill. As smoke permeated the halls and flames rapidly spread through the building, the students' jokes about fire drills ended. Two resident advisors quickly called the fire department. They pounded on doors to evacuate the dormitory. Students ran down the halls to get outside.

"It was dramatic, watching the dorm go down in flames," one student later recalled. "The fire burned a hole straight up through the dorm. It reached the roof." A staff member of William & Mary's administration could see the glow of flames from his home more than a mile away.

After the fire, reporters used the term "gutted" to describe the damage to the dormitory. Its residents lost almost everything. "The most painful thing involved hearing stories of things students lost that they could never retrieve again," a William & Mary official said. "Photographs, letters, and messages from family and friends, prized possessions, all of their academic materials—this made it very hard for some students to pick up the routine of college life again." Years later, when viewing photographs of the fire, one observer recalled, "To me, the most poignant image features the top of someone's dresser, strewn with such personal belongings as underwear, shaving cream, toothbrushes, and records covered in broken plaster from the ceiling. ... You can really sense the urgency with which students evacuated the building."

Jefferson Hall was named for William & Mary's most famous alumnus. Opened as a women's dormitory in 1920, it was sixty-three years old at the time of the fire. Costing almost $200,000 in 1920s dollars (the equivalent of nearly $2.6 million in 2020) and measuring 200 feet long by 41 feet wide, it played a special role among William & Mary's dormitories. Initially it contained a gymnasium and a small swimming pool. For many years, not only women's basketball games but also student dances were held in this gymnasium.

What caused the fire? The state fire marshal traced the fire to a faulty refrigerator cord. The flames spread via exhaust fans up and across the building. Contrary to Virginia law, the contractor had omitted the fire stops—flame-resistant material placed around electrical conduits and pipes. Without them, the flames spread rapidly. Five fire departments came to the assistance of the Williamsburg Fire Department. They fought the blaze in 14-degree temperature—so cold that gloves froze to hoses and Williamsburg's fire chief had to be treated for frostbite.

The firefighters pumped a million gallons of water, but at four o'clock in the morning, they had to declare Jefferson Hall unsalvageable.

The primary concern of firefighters was to extinguish the blaze. The primary concern of the administration of William & Mary was to ensure student safety. When the initial headcounts taken outside the dormitory indicated that some students who lived there were missing, resident advisors wrapped towels around their heads and went into the burning building. At the same time, an alert firefighter saw a shadow moving on an upper floor of the dormitory. When an aerial ladder was quickly moved to that room, firefighters found two male students who had just awakened and helped them from the building.

Many of Jefferson Hall's residents fled to adjacent Barrett Hall. Others scattered all over campus to bunk with friends. A few whose families lived close to campus drove home. The flight of residents from the immediate area made William & Mary's task of tracking them down difficult. But after a series of telephone calls and television announcements, William & Mary administration located all residents of Jefferson Hall by eleven o'clock that morning. The relief was great; no student perished in the fire. Only at 1 p.m.— twelve hours after the fire started—did Williamsburg's fire department declare it extinguished. A week later, the water in the dormitory's basement remained waist deep.

For some time after the fire, William & Mary housed the displaced students in two campus dormitories. Subsequently they moved them to Colonial Williamsburg's Motor House, which was 1.4 miles away from campus. William & Mary also leased the Commonwealth Inn (1 mile from campus) and moved students into it. Undergraduates lived in the inn—which they named "Jefferson West"—for two years until Jefferson Hall reopened. To get the one-hundred-plus students to and from campus and classes, the university had to add to its bus service. Although the students of Jefferson West tried to return quickly to normal campus life, living at Commonwealth Inn presented a series of obstacles. The motel housed only 135 of the 183 students; others had to live elsewhere. The inn lacked a kitchen and laundry facilities. It would not allow refrigerators or stoves to be moved in, so the students had to dine in the campus cafeterias. William & Mary placed phones in the halls and provided the inn's rooms with additional furniture.

The Williamsburg community immediately responded to the students' needs. So many donations of clothing arrived that the university gave a truckload of excess garments to charity. Dry cleaners cleaned students' garments free of charge, opticians replaced lost or broken glasses, and the Red Cross provided money for books and clothes. A leading merchant led a drive to raise money to assist affected students. Years later, a William & Mary vice president remembered the community's response, noting, "This action said to young students who had lost almost everything: 'There is hope here. There is a way you're going to recover.'"

The Jefferson Hall fire was Williamsburg's second-worst fire of the twentieth century. Only the burning of Phi Beta Kappa Hall in 1953 exceeded it. A William & Mary administrator who was at the center of the response to the Jefferson Hall fire later ranked it as the "most traumatic event of my time at the college."

Back on that cold January morning in 1983, the faculty wife stood looking across Jamestown Road at the burned dormitory. A professor who lived several blocks from the campus came down the street. Like her, he had been associated with William & Mary for decades. Seeing the fire equipment and smoldering building for the first time, he asked the faculty wife in astonishment what had happened. When she explained it to him, he stood looking at the ruined dormitory for some time.

"Makes you want to cry," he finally said.

"I already have," she replied.

14. Wayward Actors and Passion Plays

"One of the bonuses of live theater," a retired director of the William & Mary Theatre reflects, "is theatrical mishaps. People are always interested in theatrical mishaps. We call them 'student-induced events.'" The director continues, "My job is to avoid such incidents, but that isn't always possible. Our student staff member did once manage to catch Phi Beta Kappa Hall on fire when the wadding in a blank-firing rifle caught fire. By the time I sprinted backstage, a student was standing over a smoking piece of scenery holding a dripping fire extinguisher."

Another "student-induced event" in the theater's history occurred because the student was in jail.

At that time, the William & Mary Theatre was staging Tony Richardson's modern verse translation of the York Passion Play. A powerful drama of medieval origin, a passion play depicts the suffering and death—the Passion—of Jesus Christ. Using an updated version of a fifteenth-century script written in alliterative rhymed verse, the director of William & Mary Theatre had reset the York Passion Play in western Virginia. During the play, its characters move through the audience, and the audience becomes part of the story.

The play was scheduled for evening performances on Thursday, Friday, and Saturday, with a matinee on Sunday. Following the Saturday evening performance, the cast and crew held a private party. At the party, one cast member, of legal age, drank too much alcohol. Since he was a serious and responsible person, he decided it would not be

wise to drive his car back to his residence. Instead, he knocked on the door of a nearby apartment where he thought a student friend lived. To his confusion, an irate citizen answered the door. There was no pacifying the homeowner. This was late Saturday night, when college kids acted up and woke up the neighborhood. The irate citizen called the Williamsburg Police Department.

The police took the student actor to Williamsburg's jail and booked him. They allowed him one phone call. Clearly the alcohol was still having an effect, since the student called the William & Mary ticket office. That might have been a good plan to reach fellow thespians, except that William & Mary's ticket office—like most other ticket offices in the world—was closed at two o'clock in the morning. It would open again only an hour before the matinee performance.

On weekends the wheels of justice in Williamsburg move slowly. When the actor failed to appear an hour before the 2 p.m. matinee on Sunday, a call of alarm went out to the theater staff. In the hour that remained before the curtain went up, the staff—led by the director, the student assistant director, and the student stage manager—searched through the campus and town. They searched not only his dormitory but also Paul's Deli, the College Deli, and the Green Leafe Cafe. Since the actor was an upperclassman and viewed by others as highly responsible, the staff feared the worst. They were more worried about him than angry about his absence.

The actor was particularly important to the passion play, since he literally knew the ropes. In one of his roles, he portrayed a principal worker at Calvary. He and his fellow workers raised a 12-foot cross, with an actor depicting Jesus of Nazareth attached to the top with ropes. With the performance nearing and the wayward actor still missing, the director substituted a stagehand in the role. He quickly instructed the stagehand on how to handle the ropes. But it was a complicated procedure to learn in a limited time. The stagehand went on stage knowing the flow of the play, but literally not "all the ropes." He performed with a script in his hands.

During the play, the 100-pound cross holding aloft the 200-pound actor playing Jesus had almost reached its apogee. But then, in a series of jerks, its ropes gave way, and the cross fell slowly down to the stage floor. Several actors shrieked, and some in the audience gasped. The actor portraying Jesus was in some danger, for at one point during the unexpected descent he was dangling 10 feet in the air head down.

The director was about to step in and stop the play, but the actors—still in character—put their heads together, solved the technical problem, and quickly reelevated the cross. The show went on with its main actor drenched in nervous sweat. When the director had revised his script of the passion play, he had especially desired to evoke reactions from the audience—but not, he later declared to an interviewer, *that* kind of reaction.

Years later, the director, now retired from William & Mary, reflected that the student meant well when he knocked on a nearby apartment door looking for a bed. To have driven his car home while intoxicated would have been irresponsible. But, the retired director declared, "Responsible student behavior does not always produce desired results." Or, to put it another way, "The road to Sheol is paved with good intentions."

15. The Four-Year Roommate Lunch

In college, freshman roommates occasionally end up living together for all four years as undergraduates. In April or May of every year, the president of William & Mary invites such students to a special lunch held in the Great Hall of the Wren Building. All roommates who have roomed together in campus dorms for four years receive invitations. The president presides and addresses the group at the beginning of the luncheon. The seating for the event is round tables, and the president sits at one. The four-year roommates at his table usually discuss a broad range of topics with him. After lunch, individual photographs are taken of the president and each set of roommates. The photos are sent to the roommates after the event.

In the spring of 2007, two seniors who lived in Chandler Hall received an invitation to the lunch. Both were natives of Virginia's Shenandoah Valley. They had known each other since high school, when both attended Governor's School—but they had only been acquaintances. When each learned that the other had been admitted to William & Mary on early decision, they decided—on the spot—

to become roommates. The two freshmen were assigned to DuPont Hall. Named after a philanthropist and daughter of an alumnus, it housed almost three hundred freshmen. "Life in DuPont Dorm was characterized by extreme camaraderie," one roommate recalls. "Doors to individual rooms were almost never closed, and I recall a sense that I was always free to wander into someone's room and chat with them for as long as I wanted. Everyone had nicknames. The main foyer of the dorm, nicknamed the Pit, and its fireplace was a center of social activity."

During that first year, the two roommates learned of the four-year roommate lunch. Throughout the remaining years of college, the challenge of whether they would be eligible for the lunch when they graduated in 2007 lingered in their minds. But as often happens, the two roommates became fast friends. In four years they shared

not only a dormitory room, but also countless meals, an extended group of friends, and even rides to and from Williamsburg and their homes during the holiday breaks. At the end of the freshman year, the two participated in the annual housing lottery and were able to choose their dormitory room for the next year on the basis of a randomly assigned number. They chose a first-floor suite (a room with an adjoining semiprivate bath) in Chandler Hall—a dormitory built in an era when college dorms tended to be more spacious. The two roommates remained in that suite until graduation three years later. While the location was convenient to departmental classrooms for the roommate who majored in geology, it was less convenient for the roommate who majored in religious studies and minored in dance. But the suite was so exceptional the two roommates think they probably would have accepted it if it were located down US-60 and out of town.

Three years in the same housing allowed the roommates to pull together a living space that became almost legendary on William & Mary's campus. Starting with crown molding and ceilings over 11 feet high, they added a luxurious deep green carpet upcycled from their parents. They also added salvaged road signs, including one that named the street on which one of the student's family lived. They carried in an enormous log (5.5 feet long and 10 inches in diameter) from a campus tree felled by Hurricane Isabel. The word "TRIBE" was carved into its bark.

The decorations, in the words of one roommate, were "delightfully eclectic." They included posters for sports cars, an oil painting obtained by one roommate on a trip to the Bahamas, a scene from a ballet, and miscellaneous William & Mary memorabilia. LED lights rimmed the suite's crown molding. One roommate's notably tall loft bed rested above the door, creating a tunnel-like entrance to the room. In their first year in the suite, the two roommates won a contest for the best-decorated dorm room. They used their award, a $50 gift certificate, to purchase a chandelier for the suite. "Thereby," one roommate adds, "we ensured our victory in any future best-decorated dorm room contests." For three years, anyone who walked on the brick pathways that ran past Chandler Dorm could see the chandelier, the LED lights, and some of the suite.

During their senior year, the two roommates looked forward to the four-year roommate lunch for weeks. They decided to dress alike for the lunch and persuaded two women friends who were also "four-year-roommates" to do so as well. The two men wore blue shirts, red ties, and dark trousers. The two women wore matching dresses. The matching garb was intended as a joke for President Gene Nichol, who was well known for his sense of humor. At the lunch, President Nichol sat in the center of a single long table and discussed a wide range of topics with the fifteen to twenty students who attended. "President Nichol did an excellent job of engaging everyone present," one roommate remembers. "It felt like a lively group conversation, not a series of interviews."

Today, one of the roommates remembers the four-year roommate lunch of 2007 so well that he can still recall the dishes served. "The best-cooked polenta I've ever had," he declares. The other roommate recalls neither the food nor the conversation. But he sees the luncheon as "the culmination of my life's greatest friendship."

Following graduation, one roommate served with AmeriCorps in Philadelphia and then with the Peace Corps in Azerbaijan. He now lives in New York City and has charge of a division of a hedge fund. The other roommate went on to graduate school and then worked as a petroleum geologist in Texas before moving back to Virginia to work in the clean energy industry. In 2013 one roommate served as the other's best man for his wedding in the Wren Chapel. More than a decade after their graduation from William & Mary, the roommates remain close friends.

16. The First Black Phi Beta Kappa

As a family, his branch of the tree came of age late in the spring of 1978. The family members crossed the Rubicon into a world of respect they never imagined. Eighteen years old and sitting in an elegant and historic room, the young Black male was nervous about associating with these highly educated white people in this incredible room at the second-oldest college in the United States. His family comprised the only Black people the audience. He felt not only small but also, at the same time, ashamed of feeling that way. For moral support, he turned constantly toward his parents and oldest brother.

From the row in front of where his family was seated, a white woman kept half turning, quickly stealing disbelieving and even angry glances at the Black family. Her stares did not help ease his discomfort. Maybe, his mother later considered, maybe she thought they were the help who had come to join the celebration. What the Black family did know for sure, on the basis of their many combined years of professional Blackness, was that the woman was highly offended, believing their presence was tarnishing this glorious day in her life.

The Black teen's father was a small farmer, a Virginian born and raised across the James River in Smithfield. He was the oldest of eleven children, growing up in the midst of Jim Crow, surviving in the American South. His father was smart and eventually entered Virginia State University, a historically Black college. He dreamed of becoming a dentist. However, a farming accident required that he leave college after a year to come home to help work the family farm. His dreams of advanced education quickly became a distant longing. Although the family roots of the teenager's mother lay in Smithfield, she was a city girl, having grown up in Philadelphia. She too was an excellent student, but college was not in her future. After high school, she went directly to work, helping to take care of herself as well as her mother, who worked as a domestic for several wealthy families.

In the great migration, when numerous Black families fled the South, many of the Smithfield-based families moved to Philadelphia. The young man's father would often drive his mother north to see her sisters. On one such trip, he met a nineteen-year-old young woman. Two years later, after they married, she left the city to move to the very rural farmland of Smithfield. Within the next years, they had three boys. They promised each other that their children would obtain the education that had eluded them—the education they knew in their hearts was the key to the promise of unaccustomed accomplishments.

His father worked the land; his mother worked the boys' minds. In Smithfield, she took a job as a teacher in a church-run kindergarten, where she and a friend felt it was their duty to prepare African American children for a changing world. The two women taught with patience, love, and a firm belief in the extraordinary capabilities of their students. They demanded that their students believe the same. And they did, even at that young age. The boys studied. They wrote. They did math. They had history lessons. And most left kindergarten already knowing how to read when they walked into their first-grade classrooms. Teachers at the segregated public elementary schools coveted the graduates of Martha James Memorial Kindergarten. The mother and father continued their children's education at home. The parents went over their lessons daily. They made sure the boys did their homework, and when necessary, they stepped in to guide the children. What they felt the curriculum lacked, they made up for at home. They also made sure the boys helped each other. A shared work ethic became part of who they were as a family, and the parents consistently led the way. At every turn, they let the boys know that they were in this game with them. They worked at the elementary school when they could, with the father eventually becoming president of the PTA. They went to every parent-teacher conference. They raised money and their hands whenever something needed to be done. They lived this dream of education. The three brothers fed from it, becoming excellent students and unfaltering advocates for each other. On the eve of the final exam in physics, one brother came home from college just to help drill his younger brother and his best friends in the subject that he had come to love.

And when their mother decided to go back to school, they rallied around her. When it looked like this whole education thing might be too expensive, his father went to work at one of the meatpacking plants in Smithfield to supplement the family income. How could the boys not believe? When one of the brothers was a senior in high school, a fellow classmate asked if he were going on to college. The brother, who had never pondered such a question, responded almost innocently, "You mean there's another choice?" There wasn't another choice, not in their home.

The Phi Beta Kappa Society is the oldest and most venerated academic honor society in the United States. It dates back to 1776. Its first chapter was formed on the campus of William & Mary. And

that is where the mother, father, and oldest and youngest brothers sat on that day in the spring of 1978. This particular gathering was to celebrate the newly elected members of that year's class. When the doors to the stage opened and the honors graduates walked through them, the middle brother was first. The younger brother tried, but he could not see the look on the face of the woman who sat in front of them. In any event, she was no longer stealing glances back at them. To this day, he still wishes he could have seen what the vision of his brother, at the head of the white students, did to her.

That brother was the only Black William & Mary student in the room that day. It was an extraordinary moment when the family stood with two of the society's officers. One smiled as he said the words, "We want you to know that Brian is the first of his kind in the history of the college to receive this honor." That the professor did not seem to know how to refer to an African American elected to Phi Beta Kappa created a little awkwardness, but the members chatted amiably and shook all of their hands. At that moment, at least in that room, the family from Smithfield was looked upon as intellectual equals.

None ever looked back. The middle brother became a world-renowned religious scholar with fifteen published books to his name. His book *Revelation: A Commentary* was named by the Academy of Parish Clergy as the best reference book of 2009. Another book, *Invasion of the Dead*, was included in the academy's Top Ten Books for 2014. He is now presiding as the first African American president of historic Union Presbyterian Seminary in Richmond, Virginia. Years later, when his niece visited William & Mary as a prospective student, she found her uncle's name and the historical significance of his election in a brochure. She swelled with pride.

17. The Order of the White Jacket

At a meeting of William & Mary's class ambassadors—alumni who volunteer to contact classmates and encourage them to contribute financially to the college—the conversation centered on ways to make college more affordable.

"I can't tell you how many times a prospective applicant has asked me if William & Mary provided help to students to meet their financial obligations," said one class ambassador from the early '70s who had gone on to teach in public and private high schools for over forty years.

The former teacher's tablemates displayed interest in hearing how the teacher replied to this very real concern. The teacher explained that William & Mary had job opportunities available throughout its many departments. Students could apply for all kinds of jobs, ranging from secretarial support to ushering, working in the cafeteria, or assisting in the cleaning services. In addition, since William & Mary sits in the middle of one of America's most popular tourist spots, job opportunities were plentiful in the various colonial restaurants and taverns located around the college.

"And then I would personalize the experience for them," continued the teacher. "I would share my experiences as a student who had to work in order to attend William & Mary." The former teacher was one of eight children raised by parents of modest means. Financing four years of college for eight children would require sacrifices from all. The parents pledged to pay as much as possible, with the understanding that each child would have to work to pay the difference and to cover any extra expenses, including expenditures for social activities. The former teacher shared with the students that while at William & Mary he held a variety of jobs. During football and basketball games, he worked in the press area. He ushered at and cleaned up after concerts. He refereed football and basketball games for the college intramural program. In addition, he was a janitor at his fraternity house. But when he talked to students, he always made it clear that his favorite job during college was working as a member of the Order of the White Jacket (OWJ).

The OWJ consists of students who work not only as waitstaff for college functions but also for private events hosted by college officials. While working, they wear the traditional garb of waitstaff—black slacks, white shirts, black ties, and white jackets. Student servers are a fixture at dinners and receptions held in campus buildings, in the president's house, or in the homes of professors. Sometimes the work is tedious. The pay can run from "just OK" to "very good." But securing a place in the OWJ can be a real feather in the cap of any undergraduate who needs work. Membership of the OWJ brings students much more than financial gain. Equally important is the role that the OWJ plays in bringing students from all over campus together. OWJ members inevitably have different majors, are involved in different social or athletic organizations, and live in different dormitories or even off-campus. In addition, the OWJ places servers at events where they often interact with administrators and professors in a more personal way than experienced in the classroom. Because of these types of interactions, important—even lifelong—relationships develop between members of the OWJ and college professors and officials. Diners and servers alike shared many memories from these events over the years.

"At one of the dinners I worked," the former teacher recalled, "William & Mary's president hosted the governor of Virginia in the Great Hall of the Wren Building. When the dinner was over, the servers carried out coffee and dessert. One overeager server, working his first event, tripped on the rug. He spilled coffee not only across the tabletop but also onto the lap of the governor," the teacher continued. "For one very long moment, everyone in the room was quiet. As for the server, he was frozen in fear."

"Thankfully," the teacher declared, "the governor quickly recovered and began to chuckle at the situation. At that point, William & Mary's president exhaled a sigh of relief. Everyone joined in the laughter. The young server was able to breathe again. He withdrew from the room muttering a steady stream of apologies." The teacher concluded, "That night became a special memory for all of us."

As the former teacher pointed out, "It was really cool to be in the Order of the White Jacket." The job opportunities on campus and around Williamsburg provide help for students short on money. But it would be very difficult to exaggerate the importance of the OWJ. Not only did the job help pay bills, but the association with other OWJ members provided a different aspect of William & Mary life than the more routine experiences of class, library, or lab.

18. Following Her Idol

Beginning with its first season in 1981, the William & Mary women's soccer team played thirty-six consecutive seasons with a winning record. One soccer alum remembers growing up in Virginia during the late 1980s. Her idol was a high school soccer star from her hometown in Virginia who went on to accept a scholarship at William & Mary. She describes her idol as "fiercely competitive and ultra-talented, but also kind, accessible, a great teammate, and remarkably humble."

In middle school, the soccer player visited Williamsburg during spring break. During the visit, she and her father walked down Duke of Gloucester (DOG) Street. A girl ran toward them wearing a W&M Soccer shirt. When her dad recounts this story, as he loves to do, he emphasizes that she said, "Look, Daddy, that's gonna be me. I'm going to be wearing that shirt, running down the road."

As a senior in high school, wrestling with the decision of which college soccer program she wanted to join, the memory of that visit tugged at her. Could it be fate? she wondered. Apparently, it was. She joined the Tribe during the sweltering heat of August 1996. Today she says, "It's one of the best decisions I ever made."

Four years later, the alum earned a bachelor of arts degree, majoring in information technology and minoring in sociology. She mentions two favorite professors, one in business and one in sociology. "They seemed to really get me," she says. "I took several classes under each of them, and they wrote letters of recommendation when I later applied to law school. Both referred to me as a 'spitfire.'"

Her legendary coach, John "JD" Daly, led the William & Mary team to four straight NCAA conference championships, four trips to the NCAA tournament. In addition, the team went twice to the Sweet 16 (the top sixteen teams in the NCAA tournament) and once to the Elite 8 (the top eight teams). Daly coached from 1987 through 2017. In 2019, the player's entire 1997 team was inducted into the William & Mary Hall of Fame. Several of her teammates became individual Hall of Fame inductees. Several are also "on deck" for the honor.

The student spent the summers of her college years playing in travel leagues and teaching at soccer camps. She spent two of the summers in Portland, Oregon, playing for a league sponsored by Adidas. She describes the experiences as two of the most fun summers of her life. "I got to befriend a bunch of girls who were otherwise college and club team rivals," she recalls. "It was just awesome to hang out for two summers in furnished apartments, play soccer, and check out Oregon on Adidas's dime."

Soccer was her major activity in college. While receiving what she calls a "world-class education" at William & Mary, she also developed close ties with her sorority sisters. "For all of our collective on-field excellence," she says, "the Tribe family tree is even more impressive off-field, for our reach is broad and its influence is overwhelmingly positive." Multiple teammates, she relates, served as bridesmaids in her wedding. These teammates continue to gather regularly for reunions and group trips. Although they represent diverse backgrounds, thought, and even humor, they consistently support one another in good times and tough times. Even their parents and brothers remain close. The former player describes Tribe Soccer as "literally the best part of having gone to W&M." In 2017, the entire soccer program organized a thirty-five-year celebration. Well over a hundred alumnae attended. The alum says, "We know how to throw a party!"

Individually, she vowed to follow in her idol's footsteps. She did that by being a three-time All-American and by setting Tribe scoring records. She was named William & Mary Female Athlete of the Year in 1999–2000, and she twice earned finalist ranking for the Hermann Trophy, the most prestigious individual award in college soccer. She was a Honda Award finalist in 1999.

In 2011, she joined her idol in the William & Mary Hall of Fame. Her idol's response was a bouquet of flowers with a note saying, "You're my hero now." She declares, "Don't tell me that isn't an idol worthy of worship."

19. The Founding of the Black Student Organization

In the 1960s, William & Mary experienced a reinvigoration in its physics department. Its faculty reached a significant agreement with the National Aeronautics and Space Administration (NASA). They would manage NASA's research laboratory in Newport News in return for studying space radiation through the use of a proton cyclotron. This laboratory's name was the Space Radiation Effects Laboratory (SREL). At the time, NASA was concerned about the effects of space radiation on living tissue and vehicle equipment while they were in Earth's orbit. The opportunities to engage in cutting-edge research in Virginia attracted many physicists to William & Mary. These physicists educated an array of new PhDs who studied not only nuclear physics but also plasma, atomic, and solid-state physics. William & Mary's physics program grew to such an extent that it awarded its first PhD degree in 1967.

In the meantime, an undergraduate from Washington, DC, was finishing a major in mathematics at Morgan State University, as well as completing a second major in physics. His mentors in both departments encouraged him to apply for graduate school in physics. When he did apply, William & Mary offered him a full fellowship for graduate study, a requisite for continuing his education with a new wife and a first child on the way. In the fall of 1968, the graduate of Morgan State arrived in Williamsburg accompanied by his young wife and month-old son. As one of twelve new graduate students in physics at William & Mary, he began to settle into the environment of the physics department. The new graduate student soon discovered that he was the lone African American among William & Mary's physics students and faculty. He also found that he was one of the few African American students on William & Mary's campus.

To this point in his life, the student's contact with integration had been minimal. His mother had been one of a few African Americans in her high school in Evanston, Illinois. He himself had attended fourth grade in a newly desegregated public school in Washington, DC, but "white flight" had occurred so swiftly that the school essentially remained all-black. The student's wife also had been educated only in segregated schools. In Williamsburg, the family rented a house one block from campus. Despite their proximity to campus, he and his wife felt isolated. Although the student himself owned and drove a Volkswagen "Bug," his wife could not drive and stayed home with their baby. In the 1960s, many college students became involved first in the civil rights movement and then in the antiwar movement that emerged from the Vietnam War. Many activists did not see war and social justice as mutually exclusive issues. Their joint effort created more of a united front. Multiple demonstrations against the war occurred on William & Mary's campus. At the same time, the students were struggling to persuade William & Mary's administration to acknowledge the school's troubled racial history. Almost before the new graduate student knew it, he found himself in the middle of these two national movements as they played out at William & Mary. He quickly rose to become the leader of a local movement—that of creating a Black Student Organization (BSO) on campus.

In the fall of 1969, a coalition of Black students and a handful of white students won over some formerly reluctant William & Mary administrators. The students received permission to establish a constitution and formal bylaws for a BSO on campus. The student participated in writing both the constitution and bylaws. The BSO's first efforts at William & Mary focused on eliminating the display of Confederate battle flags around the campus. Given what the flags stood for, the BSO argued, they were unfit for a distinguished institution of higher education.

Even as the campus reacted to the deaths occurring from protests elsewhere in the nation, support from William & Mary faculty and students increased. In 1970 under its president's leadership, the BSO

joined nationwide demonstrators protesting four deaths at the hands of the National Guard at Kent State University and two deaths by city and state police at Jackson State University. Compared to such campuses as Michigan, Yale, or Berkeley, the level of protests at William & Mary was tranquil. When Richard Nixon visited campus during his 1968 presidential campaign, for example, he was greeted not with jeers and boos, but with a sea of signs carrying such messages as "'Nixon's the One': One *what*?"

On campus, senior administrators became numb as student protests continued to increase. This was especially the case when the graduate student himself caused headlines by calling the sitting president of William & Mary "a bigot." Before he came to William & Mary, the president had been Virginia's superintendent of public instruction during the legislature's opposition to the federally mandated integration of public schools, known as "Massive Resistance." The president, a native Virginian and a William & Mary alumnus, had blocked the creation of the BSO in 1969 on the basis that it focused only on one race.

As demonstrations escalated, the physics graduate student had placed himself and his family in the middle of very uncertain times. He was living in Old Virginia while stirring things up—actions that terrified both his wife and mother. Despite the explosive environment, the physics graduate student forged friendships with a number of white students. Having white students chartered into the BSO threw a wrench into arguments of the president of William & Mary against forming a club that admitted only members of one race. And so the president relented.

With the completion of degree requirements for a master of science in physics, the student left William & Mary in May 1970. It was the first

Students attend a Black Student Organization meeting. *Photo Courtesy of University Archives, Special Collections Research Center, William & Mary Libraries*

time he had left Williamsburg since the beginning of his graduate study. Finishing all required coursework while simultaneously being a "campus radical" was no small feat. The distractions of family life and campus activism were too strong. After playing with his bright-eyed son, he studied late into the night, every night. During his first months of study, he was happy to learn that he was as academically gifted as the other graduate students. But when he took the dreaded PhD qualifying exam after his first year, he failed it. The academic work required for the PhD conflicted with his family life. By the time he left Williamsburg in 1970, his brief marriage had ended. He settled his estranged wife and son in an apartment in the DC area. He left the Volkswagen "Bug" for his wife to drive after she received a driver's license. Although his two-year-old son wanted to go with him, the separation agreement awarded his wife custody, giving him visiting rights only. When he left the apartment, both he and his son were in tears. Shortly after leaving the apartment that night, he suffered a severe anxiety attack. Experiencing tremors, he could not breathe and came very close to convulsing.

Months passed. At one point, he was an hour away from joining the Black Panther Party in DC. The hard realization that the Panthers used guns challenged him to push for change in other ways. When the police raided the Panther headquarters in DC one evening, he was thankful he had not joined. His life could have gone in a completely different direction.

The awakening at William & Mary propelled him into a successful and eclectic life. For a year after leaving William & Mary, he taught mathematics at Bowie State University. Later, when he decided to return to William & Mary to finish his PhD, he was pleasantly surprised to learn that the department had kept his full fellowship open in the hope that he would return. Reuniting with his William & Mary community, he again took the dreaded PhD qualifying exam—but this time passed it. In 1976, he successfully completed all requirements for the PhD After receiving the PhD, his life "exploded with good things."

From William & Mary he went on to perform physics research at SUNY–Stony Brook and at the University of Paris. He presented his work and spoke widely around the globe. He sailed, painted, married a William & Mary graduate, received an honorary doctor of science degree from William & Mary, and significantly influenced the PhD program in physics at Hampton University and the building of the Jefferson Lab, which replaced SREL in Newport News. He became the founding chancellor of the University of Washington Bothell. As of this writing, he proudly serves on the Board of Visitors of William & Mary.

When one of his speaking engagements in the 1980s was at Jackson State University, he visited the dorm area where the shootings had occurred. Although twenty years had passed, the bullet holes were still visible in the brick face of the dormitory. He was overcome with grief.

20. Don't Show Them the Law School

As of the mid-1970s, William & Mary's law school existed minimally in the old Carnegie library building on the campus of William & Mary. Founded in 1779, the oldest law school in the United States, it was one of Virginia's two state-supported law schools (the University of Virginia School of Law was the other). At one time named the "Department of Jurisprudence," William & Mary's law school was renamed the "Marshall-Wythe School of Law" in 1953. John Marshall was chief justice of the United States. George Wythe taught law to Thomas Jefferson, to Marshall, and to other Founding Fathers.

For decades, the General Assembly of Virginia provided little financial support to the state's oldest law school. To be sure, as of the 1970s, many of the school's graduates were successfully practicing law all over Virginia. Its faculty included a noted graduate of William & Mary and Harvard Law School who would later become the twenty-fifth president of William & Mary. In 1950, the law faculty included a professor whom *Life* magazine recognized as one of the eight "Great Teachers" in America. But in the annual review of law schools then published by the American Bar Association, William & Mary's law school was rated poorly. In the category of financial support, it ranked in the lowest decile nationally. The consistently low and uneven funding by the legislature resulted not just in overcrowded facilities, but also in inadequate library holdings, low faculty recruitment and salaries, and an unimpressive national reputation.

In 1972, Virginia's highly regarded junior senator lost his bid for reelection. He had become noted for opposing the dominant Dixiecrat political organization in Virginia, and he had spoken out against the commonwealth's policy of "Massive Resistance" to integration. Popular in Washington with Democrats, Republicans, and journalists, he was once described as "a workhorse rather than a show horse." After the former junior senator returned to legal practice, William & Mary invited him to become dean of its school of law. The former senator's experience was extensive. Besides serving in the US Senate for six years, he had served for twelve years in the Virginia General Assembly. The appointment was wise. Not only did the new dean have wide personal contacts in Virginia and elsewhere, but he also knew how to get things done in legislative chambers. His first years were focused on raising the funding of the law school. Through lobbying in Richmond, meetings with committees of the American Bar Association, speeches, and interviews, the new dean declared publicly, and often, that the accreditation of the law school was in jeopardy because of low funding. The American Bar Association supported his arguments. Above all, the dean emphasized the need for a new law school building.

Virginia prided itself on the role it had played in the history of the United States. The dean's factual arguments, jeremiads, and woe-filled interviews raised the possibility that the oldest law school in America—one funded by the commonwealth of Virginia—could lose its accreditation. The prospect of such a calamity embarrassed the governor and legislature. And it would happen on their watch. Because of his political experience, the new dean knew exactly what

he was doing and saying. As a result of his efforts, the welfare of William & Mary's law school now became a high priority for the general assembly. By September 1976, ground had been broken on campus for a new law building. Although construction did not begin until three years after the dean began his campaign, the building was completed and opened for use in the 1980–81 academic year.

During the planning for the building, the dean expressed the desire that

William & Mary's new law school be a "superb physical facility." It was. Throughout the construction, however, the dean worried that legislators and observers alike would find the new building "opulent." The associate dean of the law school persuaded the dean to ask the general assembly for a favor. The associate argued that the dean should ask the legislators to approve highly decorative parquet floors for the lobby. In the associate dean's words, the former senator finally agreed—but "reluctantly." Once the parquet floors were authorized, the associate dean recommended that the lobby have oriental rugs on top of its ornate floors. He hoped the dean could secure the rugs as a company donation, since he knew that one of the dean's old friends was president of a prominent southern textile company. It billed itself as manufacturing "the finest power-loomed rugs in the world." For his own part, the dean assumed that his old friend, the company's chief operating officer, would automatically decline presenting an expensive gift to a law school in Virginia. When the president agreed to donate the oriental rugs to the law school, the dean was—in the associate dean's words—"surprised and discomforted."

"When the rugs arrived," the associate dean recalls, "they did indeed look beautiful on the parquet floors." To the new dean's eyes, however, they looked *opulent*. He had had extensive experience with the commonwealth of Virginia's propensity for saving money. Throughout the construction, he worried that the legislators would find the rugs and floors extravagant. Hence when the construction was completed and the dean learned that a committee of the general assembly was coming to inspect the new building, he said to William & Mary's president, only half jokingly, "Don't show them the law school."

"Ever after," the associate dean remembers, "whenever a legislative delegation arrived at the law school, the dean would tell them right off, 'I know that you are probably looking at those oriental rugs. Let me assure you that not a single penny of state money was spent to buy them. Not a single penny. It was all—I say *all*—paid for with private funds.'"

During the former senator's nine years as dean, William & Mary's law school steadily gained national recognition. Formerly ranking outside the top 150 law schools in the 1960s, it now ranks within the top fifty. Almost forty years after the new building opened, the "finest power-loomed rugs in the world" still grace its lobby. If the US senator turned law dean were still alive, his successor, who became president of William & Mary, declared with confidence, "I would have the satisfaction of pointing out that they turned out to be a pretty economical expenditure after all."

21. A Tradition of History

The Delaware family had a deeply rooted tradition of loving rare books and rare manuscripts. The grandfather, a noted Presbyterian minister, was a preeminent collector of such things. The grandson was one of the first students to receive a PhD in history from William & Mary. The great-grand-daughter, who inherited a love of rare books and manu-scripts, also took a PhD in history from William & Mary.

When William & Mary established its PhD program in history in 1967, the grandson was one of the first applicants. As the admissions committee recognized, he brought a special background to the study of history. He had visited rare bookstores with his grandfather from childhood on. By the eighth grade, he had a rare book collection of his own.

"He baptized me into primary sources," the student remembers of his grandfather. "If the mail arrived during lunch, he would excuse himself, read the catalog, telephone the dealer, and then return to the table." By his senior year at Dickinson College, the grandson had decided to continue his study in the graduate field of historic sites. In the 1960s, William & Mary was one of only three American institutions to offer such a program. The Cooperstown Graduate Program (associated with the State University of New York at Oneonta) and the Winterthur Program of the University of Delaware were the other two. At the time of his application, William & Mary was in the process of expanding its MA program in history into a PhD program. Therein lies a story.

From 1964 on, William & Mary already had a PhD program—in physics. In 1964, the university's president had attended a meeting of the faculty and announced that the State Council of Higher Education for Virginia had recognized the unusual quality of

William & Mary's physics department. Hence, they not only had directed that William & Mary establish a PhD program in physics but had already announced its establishment. William & Mary's faculty bylaws required that all new educational programs must have the support of a majority of the faculty. A professor who was at the meeting remembers: "The president's action, of course, circumvented what would have been a negative vote in that faculty meeting had anyone proposed that William & Mary start a PhD program. As I recall, the president's announcement had an interesting effect on the opinions of a wide range of faculty members, most of them negative."

Subsequently, several years later, when the State Council of Higher Education directed William & Mary to establish a PhD program in history, faculty approval was crucial. From the start, however, the proposed program aroused significant opposition. Most of the outspoken opposition came from two history faculty members. Citing their experiences as students at Johns Hopkins and Harvard, the two argued in speeches and in mimeographed statements that doctoral programs change an institution's mission. Instead of focusing on undergraduates, universities with PhD programs focused more, they declared, on faculty publications, graduate courses, and just generally keeping up with other PhD programs. In addition, these opponents asserted, departments awarding doctorates tended to assign their experienced faculty to teach graduate courses. Teaching assistants were then given the responsibility of teaching and grading many undergraduate courses formerly taught by seasoned faculty. As a result, undergraduate classes had become larger and larger to allow graduate courses to remain small.

A final argument against the PhD program involved William & Mary's lack of resources to support it. Over the years, Virginia's legislature had rarely supported the university's undergraduate program adequately. Why then, the opponents argued, would it adequately support an expensive PhD program? "From the very beginning," notes a retired professor, "the proposed PhD program suffered from a constraint of resources." The history department negotiated for a year with the university administration. The department insisted that nationally competitive salaries, sabbaticals for faculty, increased library budgets, and graduate fellowships were necessities before the program could be established. "The administration would ... agree ... to the proposals," the professor remembers. "But when the time came, it would not provide the promised money."

Faculty in other departments became increasingly wary of the proposed program. The mood on campus indicated that most William & Mary faculty still believed that high-quality undergraduate work was at the heart of the university. But the power lay with the legislature and the administration, and gradually the university faculty—which included a number of new members—came to favor the PhD program. Thus, in 1967, the proposal received a majority vote from the faculty. Virginia's oldest institution of higher education added another doctoral-level course to its curriculum and appointed a highly regarded American historian to head the program.

This period of internal contention and tension marked a low point for the Department of History. The story has a happy ending, for in later years many of its students enthusiastically supported the doctoral program. Among the first applicants accepted was the student from Delaware. In later years, he praised the PhD program. "One of the things that made it great," he declared, "was that, within limits, graduate students in history could take any undergraduate course listed by the department. In addition, they could take courses offered in the Institute of Early American History and Culture." Founded by William & Mary and Colonial Williamsburg, the Institute of Early American History and Culture (now the Omohundro Institute) supported research into early American history and published the prestigious *William & Mary Quarterly*. "In sum," the alumnus declares today, "the scholars and material on early American history available to graduate students at William & Mary in the 1960s were better than those at any institution in the country."

The alumnus also points out that PhD candidates took classes from excellent professors, virtually all of whom continued to teach undergraduate classes. "William & Mary could stand on its own with any institution in the nation," he declares. "There were lots of good professors on its campus." Fifty years later, the alumnus still remembers three faculty—one in Southern history, the others in English history—as "the greatest lecturers ever." He describes one as "a professor's professor." The alumnus continues, "Taken together, these professors were *spectacular*. They were very much of their time and place. That is, they were very good scholars. But they were also oriented toward excellence in classroom lecturing. When appropriate, they were willing to use theatrics. I remember them fondly. For them, teaching was an art."

The alumnus wrote his master's thesis on colonial South Carolina. He wrote his PhD dissertation on reform movements in the South between 1780 and 1830. His dissertation—at 565 pages, one of the longest ever written by a graduate student at William & Mary—took him to sixty libraries. While writing his dissertation, the student applied for the position of curator of manuscripts at the William L. Clements Library in Michigan, one of the great research libraries in America. He had been introduced to the library years ago by his grandfather. When he was offered the position, the alumnus accepted. In the world of rare books and manuscripts, he quickly became known as the first person in the nation to pick up a phone and place an order when a catalog arrived.

Five years after being appointed curator of manuscripts, the William & Mary alumnus was selected as the Clements Library's third director. During his tenure, the library's collections essentially doubled. It added American social history to its major collections of American political and military history. Materials dealing with the Civil War and slavery became even more important. When the new director encountered a collection for sale that he thought indispensable to the library, he would purchase the papers and then raise the money to pay for them. The director emphasized visual materials, created

a print division, and established an extensive photographic collection. Under his leadership, the Clements Library began actively serving undergraduate classes and undergraduate researchers. When the director retired after thirty years, the library had developed into one of the most important research centers in the United States. "You couldn't find a place more fun to work in," he said at his retirement.

The story does not end there. Years later, the graduate's daughter followed in her father's footsteps. From age eight on, riding in her family car with a map spread out on her lap, she visited bookstores and historic sites on Saturdays and holidays with her father. With a mother who taught history, a grandfather who studied Greek in his retirement, and a family that had frequent scholarly conversation at the dinner table, she imbibed her family's enthusiasm for historical artifacts and culture. Like her father and mother, she attended William & Mary. After finishing a master's degree in the prestigious Winterthur program in Delaware, she took her graduate work in American history, as her mother and father had, at William & Mary. After receiving her PhD in history from William & Mary, she promises—with several decades ahead before she retires—to have a future similar to that of her great-grandfather , father, and mother. She now holds a university chair in decorative arts and material culture at Winterthur. History is in the marrow of her bones.

Should William & Mary—essentially an undergraduate school—have started a PhD program in history? "William & Mary deserved to have a PhD program," the retired library director declares today. "It could do as fine a job as any place. Those who wanted to start the program had vision." His daughter agrees. "At William & Mary I learned to make a classroom of the world of historic sites and landscapes," she says. "William & Mary and its history program are remarkable. The commitment to teaching not only content and the art of historical scholarship, but also the art of teaching and pedagogy, is truly rare."

II. FACULTY LIFE AT WILLIAM & MARY

22. George's

When the young instructor joined the faculty in August, she was pleased to learn she could rent an apartment in Colonial Williamsburg's Merchant Square. Only a block from campus, the apartment was on the second floor of a building that also housed an ice cream store, a paper expression or plaque store, and a restaurant named the Campus Restaurant but known to locals as George's.

For much of the new instructor's first semester of teaching, George's Restaurant became a kind of base. After her 9 a.m. class, she would often buy a copy of the *New York Times* at Williamsburg Drugs, take it into George's, sit in the back corner booth, and contentedly read with her late breakfast. For her, George's provided a moment of peace in a rushed day. If she was not cooking or going out that evening, it was also where she typically had dinner.

Stories circulated at William & Mary about the rules George dictatorially imposed in his restaurant. One, witnessed by two faculty members, occurred when a family of four from France chose George's as a place to have lunch. When the family took their seats and began to converse, George, wielding a spatula in one hand, yelled, "This America, you speak English." The new instructor, however, viewed her relationship with George as neighborly, and in any case, she spoke English.

But one morning, after she asked for a refill of her coffee, George turned from the stove and shouted, "No second cup. Only one cup." Stunned, the instructor looked across the room at a glowering George and said, "I ... beg ... your ... pardon?"

George replied emphatically, "Too many cups of coffee." Quickly placing money on the table to cover her bill, the instructor was out of the restaurant and walking on Prince George Street in less than sixty seconds.

She stayed away from the restaurant for four months. But when winter was turning to spring, she left her morning class and entered George's. She took her old seat in the familiar corner booth. She expected some kind of neighborly welcome. In addition, she assumed that George would have learned a lesson about politeness after his coarseness caused him to lose her business.

During breakfast she did not read a newspaper, since she had learned from students that George now prohibited reading while eating. But she did order a second cup of coffee from Mary, his wife and waitress. "George doesn't allow that," Mary replied. Overhearing the order, George shouted, "No second cup." The instructor immediately walked out of the restaurant.

George's was a Williamsburg original for almost thirty years. Every college town has a place like this. Unadorned walls; nine booths on one side, kitchen and counter on the other; students or unwary tourists sitting at the tables; jukeboxes constantly playing American or Greek music; George—described by a student as "a bald little man in a gravy-stained apron ... seemingly perpetually angry, standing at the stove and sometimes muttering in Greek." And his wife, Mary, "roaming the narrow diner like a drill sergeant, advising everyone, 'Taste your beans before you salt them.'"

A multitude of cats loitered in the adjacent alley. Although George loathed loud talkers and slow eaters, he liked cats. George met Mary in West Virginia and came with her to Williamsburg in 1962. She was a large woman with beehive hair and a weakness for catalog shopping.

"Ah, George's!" one alumnus from the 1960s reflected. "For a mere $1.15, one could have a half pound of what George called 'ground steak,' a potato, and canned peas or string beans, plus coffee or iced tea and rice pudding for dessert."

"I remember the low price for dinner," another alumnus said. "Maybe $1.99 from 1978 to 1982. Fantastic rice pudding for dessert. And being glared at by the owner if you did not vacate your table quickly." Another former patron reported, "I remember that place as being like the 'Cheeseburger—Cheeseburger' skit on *Saturday Night Live*."

"I had a boyfriend sophomore year who actually wooed me by taking me there frequently," an alumna remembered. "Ha!" she concluded.

Ultimately, George lost his restaurant in 1987. Diagnosed later with cancer, he died in the hospital shortly thereafter. Seventy people came to his funeral. Former patrons set up a display in his living room, complete with booths, place settings, and the restaurant's neon sign.

23. Buzzing the Eiffel Tower

From the 1940s on, William & Mary's faculty was laced with veterans of World War II. One—a professor of education—flew twenty-two missions over Germany as a radio operator and gunner on a B-17 Flying Fortress. He was barely twenty years old. The Flying Fortress was the American warplane that inflicted immense damage on Nazi Germany.

On May 7 and 8, 1945, Germany surrendered, and the war in Europe ended. On the following morning, the commanding officer of the Army Air Corps base in England ordered his pilots to make low-level flights over Europe. One of the reasons for the flights was to show Allied crews the effect their daily bombing had on bringing about peace.

When the plane—named by its crew "Something for the Boys"—took off from England, the crew were in a jubilant mood. No longer would they have to arise at 2 a.m. to fly through thick antiaircraft fire and bomb German cities. No longer would they return from a bombing raid with planes missing. Unless the Army Air Corps sent them to the Pacific theater to assist in the defeat of the Japanese, they had survived the war. Soon they would be back home rebuilding their lives.

As ordered, the planes flew in formation. The professor remembered that the pilot of his plane was in a "crazy" mood due to the surrender of Germany. He flew their airplane over the English Channel in great swoops—a breach of discipline. As soon as the plane cleared the Channel, however, its pilot abandoned even more of the imposed wartime discipline. He flew "Something for the Boys" over Brussels and other European cities at treetop level. The plane's crew found the streets of those liberated cities full of celebrators and exchanged waves.

When their plane reached Paris, the pilot did not fly *over* the Eiffel Tower. Instead, he stunned the crew by making a slow-banking circle *around* the tower. The professor later described their circling of the Eiffel Tower as "a fool's stunt." Over the radio, their squadron leader was even more denunciatory. He angrily described their circling of the Eiffel Tower as "foolhardy and stupid." Hence the future William & Mary professor first saw the Eiffel Tower through a gunner's window, with half of the 984-foot tower above—not below—him.

After leaving Paris, the B-17 flew so low over one French farm that its wheels would have touched the ground had they been lowered. "My God!" the future professor remembered thinking then. "Our pilots have *really* lost their senses."

When the plane crossed into Germany, the mood of the crew turned serious. In Cologne, which lost 95 percent of its population to bombing and evacuation, nothing was standing except the Roman Catholic cathedral, which had a hole in its roof. On the city's deserted streets, in the description of the professor, the Americans saw only an "old, ragged lady pulling a small wagon." In city after city in Germany, they encountered similar scenes. When they returned to their base in England, the pilot received a severe dressing-down—a "reaming" in military terminology—for the pilot's lack of discipline and "stunt" at the Eiffel Tower. Discharged from the military in 1945, the future professor used the G.I. Bill to take bachelor's, master's, and doctoral degrees. In 1958 he joined the faculty of William & Mary to teach statistics. Modest, compassionate, philanthropic, and devoted to teaching, he helped to develop and shape the School of Education. He viewed its expansion from a small department to a separate school as the crowning achievement of his career. "One of the best prepared and caring professors I studied under," a doctoral student remembered him. "He exuded care for students who were scared to death of such tough subject matter."

After the war, the professor remained in the Air Force Reserve. He rose to the rank of colonel and received significant assignments. He and his wife visited Europe four times, including Germany twice. On their first visit to Europe following the war, they went to Paris. When the couple rode the lift to the top of the Eiffel Tower, the professor told his wife: "You know, this isn't the perspective that I'm accustomed to seeing the Eiffel Tower from. I'm more accustomed to flying around it."

24. Old Highway

When the alarm sounded in her apartment in Williamsburg at six o'clock on Friday morning, the professor realized immediately that the previous evening's weather forecast had been accurate. "In early morning," the meteorologist at the Newport News TV station had declared, "snow will turn to sleet." And this was early morning.

Nevertheless, she finished packing and walked out to her car, which was starting to accumulate snow. She was scheduled to fly from Richmond International Airport to Boston to attend a conference at Harvard. The subjects of many of the papers being delivered interested her. Many leaders in her field would be there. So would faculty with whom she had studied in graduate school. As professional meetings go, it would be a kind of reunion. She was looking forward to the weekend.

Richmond International Airport is 46 miles from William & Mary. Initially, the snow and sleet seemed drivable on the interstate that connected the two cities. The snow forced her to drive slowly. But the closer she got to Richmond, the more the snow became sleet. Weather announcements steadily interrupted the NPR broadcasts on her car radio. The whole East Coast seemed to be experiencing a snowstorm. Finally, when she was creeping along about 20 miles from the airport, the announcement came. All flights to and from Richmond were canceled.

What to do? She could not make it to the meeting in Cambridge. She decided to go back to Williamsburg. The radio had just announced that William & Mary and other Tidewater schools were closing for the day. The prediction was that at some point, Williamsburg would become snowed in. She thought, "Well, I'll just spend the day at home reading and grading papers."

The return on I-64 was slow going. Cars bearing Virginia license plates crept along an average of what she guessed to be 17 miles per hour—if that. On the highway, large tractor trailers with out-of-state license plates steadily passed the slower-moving natives. In the two hours it took her to drive back to Williamsburg, the professor continually passed slower-moving cars. She saw many cars with idling motors stopped under overpasses. Every so often, a police car with flashing blue lights passed her. She counted four or five accidents, fortunately all small. The usual salt trucks were diligently at work. Businesses along the interstate were shutting off lights and closing.

As a native of Vermont, she found it difficult to keep from scoffing at some of these roadside scenes. During the winter, virtually everyone in her hometown regularly drove in this kind of weather. Parents routinely dropped the kids off at school in snowstorms. Stores rarely closed. Finally, when she saw one car holding up a line of twenty or more cars because it was going no more than 10 miles per hour, she could take it no longer. She was still 8 miles from Williamsburg, and it was plainly going to take another forty-five minutes or even an hour to get there. Pulling out her cell phone, she dialed the office number of the dean of the faculty. He had been raised in South Dakota, gone to college in Minnesota, and attended law school in Massachusetts. Snowstorm or no snowstorm—she knew he would be in his office, working.

He was. He answered the call on the first ring. In a disparaging voice, she described to him the scenes she had witnessed along the interstate—the bumper-to-bumper traffic; the lack of sufficient sand, salt, and plowing; the cars pulled over to the side waiting for the snow to stop; the accidents. The dean listened carefully. When she had finished expressing her frustration, he replied, "*Shoot!* If we had closed things down on days like this in South Dakota or Minnesota, we would've gotten nothing done from October to April."

After sharing a knowing chuckle with the dean, she drove on. She smiled as she passed car after car, even a few trucks. She felt superior. Skillful. Savvy. In charge of her environment. She was Old Highway.

25. A Norwegian Trespasser on Sunday

One Sunday morning, a professor left his house to attend church, only to find an elderly stranger in his backyard. The man was dressed in a three-piece suit and tie and wore highly polished black shoes. He appeared to be looking for something. And he was clearly trespassing. But the Lord's Prayer, which the professor would soon recite, directs Christians to "forgive us our trespasses, as we forgive those who trespass against us." So, the professor approached the elderly visitor and asked if he could help.

In accented English, the man introduced himself as "Professor Doctor Somebody," a retired science professor from the University of Oslo. To the professor, he looked like a Nobel Prize winner. The visitor said that he was staying with a scientist (also retired) who lived in the neighborhood. He was looking for a road that his host had said ran behind this house.

At this point, the William & Mary professor, pressed for time, declared that he was on his way to church. Would the Norwegian visitor possibly like to join him? "*Yes*," the visitor said immediately. The professor then said, "I attend the Church of England—what we call 'the Episcopal Church' in America. The service is similar to that of your Lutheran Church in Norway. Do you still want to attend?" Hardly had the professor finished his explanation, when the trespasser repeated another emphatic "*yes*."

Once the service started, the professor saw that his Norwegian visitor was unfamiliar with Anglican worship, which at points is identical to Lutheran worship. Although the visitor knew some of it, he displayed uncertainty about the rest. At the coffee hour following the service, the professor learned that his guest was not a native of Norway, but rather a White Russian whose parents had fled from Russia to Norway at the start of the Bolshevik Revolution. Over the decades in Oslo, he had attended a Russian Orthodox church. One member of the Episcopal congregation had a similar background. This parishioner had also been raised in Russia by a mother and father who supported the czar. But his parents had immigrated to the United States rather than to Scandinavia.

When the professor introduced the two men during coffee hour, they immediately began speaking Russian. While juggling coffee and pastries, they happily continued speaking in their native tongue for a half hour. When the professor drove the scientist back to his host's house, the visitor declared that he was delighted with the conversation he had during the coffee hour. "The church member spoke pure, classical Russian," he said. "It was beautiful," he declared. "Beautiful. It was *elegant.*"

26. The Department Chairman/Chairperson/Chair Who Erred

From the nineteenth century on, college departments in the United States were led by a *head* or *chairman*. A *head* served at the pleasure of the president of the institution and could hold office indefinitely. In contrast, a *chairman* served a set term. Once it was over, then he or she rotated out of office. In the 1960s and '70s, most American colleges and universities replaced headships with elected chairmanships. Most departmental faculties now elected their chairman for a set term— perhaps three or five years. Departments could reelect their chairman once, but then its faculty were required to elect a different successor.

Over the years the term *chairman* (viewed as too masculine) changed to *chairperson* (viewed as too lengthy) and finally to *chair*. The last term initially pleased few faculty. At first, grammatical purists satirized the new practice of calling a human being a "chair." Campuses would be the scene of conversations such as this one:

"The chair is supporting the proposal for a senior seminar."

"Oh, the chair is? Well, how about the typewriter? Or the lamp? Where do they stand on the question of a senior seminar?"

By whatever name, however, the new system seemed an improvement. It undercut the tendency of department heads to become dictatorial. Different chairs brought different leadership styles to the office. No longer was a department identified with the views of a single person. William & Mary changed from headships to department chairs in the 1970s. But the new system created new problems. Across the nation, professors increasingly proved unwilling to take on the hassles and conflicts of administering a department without also retaining some of the former power and prestige of the headships. Schools found that even their largest departments contained only two or three faculty willing to serve as chair. And usually at least some of those professors were precisely the ones whom colleagues preferred not to serve as chair.

At William & Mary, one of the science departments particularly fell into that category. Its newly elected chair held degrees from prestigious British universities. Among his colleagues he was known for diligence, personal integrity, and honesty of expression—but also for rigidity, obstinacy, and rudeness. In daily affairs, he acted as if his colleagues were not quite pulling their weight. When he was elected chair, he barely received a majority vote from his department. Nevertheless, his colleagues were grateful that he had made himself available, for no one else had.

The new chair was in his first year of office when a department member returned to her office late one afternoon. Taped to the office door, she found a white envelope. Inside the envelope was a handwritten note from the chair, stating that a student had come to his office that afternoon and registered a series of strong complaints against her. The student claimed that the professor did not know her subject, that she often canceled class, that when she did not cancel she arrived late, and that when class did meet she was rarely prepared. The chair's note directed the professor to address these problems immediately and required her to come in the next morning for a very serious conversation. "If you spent more time interacting with students," the note concluded, "I would not have to spend my time dealing with their complaints about you."

The professor's stomach sank. In a decade of teaching, she had never been the object of a complaint. In fact, she almost always overprepared for class. And she was popular with her students. Then it hit her. She looked again at the name of the course on the chair's note and at the name of the complaining student. She had never taught that course. It was entirely out of her field. She had never taught that student. She did not even know the student. In fact, another woman, a visiting professor, was teaching that particular course.

It was after five o'clock, and lights were off in all offices except that of the chair at the other end of the hall. Within ten seconds the professor was running full speed down the hall to the chair's office. She knocked but burst through the door without waiting for an invitation. Shocked, the chair froze behind his typewriter. Waving the note, the professor shouted, "I do not teach this course. I never have. I've never taught this student. I do not even know the student." The professor continued, almost in a tirade, "You want to know why you have so much trouble with your colleagues? You want to know why your enrollment is so low? It's because you shoot from the hip without thinking. That's the way you operate. That's you. I do not owe that student an apology. You owe me an apology." She stormed out of the office and went home and simmered for the rest of the evening.

The next day, the professor found a handwritten apology from the chair in her department mailbox. Following similar confrontations with other faculty, the chair—who otherwise had genuine administrative ability—decided that one term in office was enough. Afterward, he and the professor returned to their original relationship—somewhat distant, but still courteous. But some years after the incident, she confided to a colleague that she suspected that the former chair remained skeptical of her innocence.

27. The Early Morning Class

At a scholarly meeting one year, a William & Mary professor dined with an alumnus who taught at Kent State University. During dinner, the William & Mary professor asked who his tablemate's favorite professor had been as an undergraduate in Williamsburg. After reflection, the alumnus replied, "Oddly enough, it wasn't a member of my own department, History. Actually, it was the chair of the Department of Government." He then named a renowned figure on campus.

Raised on a Virginia farm, this future department chair took his bachelor of arts in political science at HampdenSydney College and his doctorate in political science at Columbia University. In those days, farm boys from Virginia did not usually end up studying at Ivy League institutions. For a time after graduation, he had worked in New York City for the famous Mayor Fiorello LaGuardia. Always characterized by a strong desire to give back what he had received, the professor taught at William & Mary from 1937 to 1966. He spent World War II in Washington.

Returning to Virginia, he became one of the reformers who worked to change both William & Mary and the segregated state of Virginia. Southern in manner, but an integrationist and a political moderate-liberal, he knew every county clerk in Virginia. The conservative Virginia establishment centered in Richmond knew him as a principal opponent. When teaching, he would open his first class of the academic year by saying in a heavy southern drawl, "I am a Virginian, a southerner, and a Democrat." He would often say, "I am viewed as a liberal in Virginia and a fascist in New York City."

"Let me give you an example of his teaching," the alumnus continued. "One winter morning, we arrived at our 8 a.m. class in the old Marshall-Wythe Building to find the windows wide open and cold air pouring in. The temperature was dropping steadily. Our professor paid no attention and started the class promptly. As his lecture proceeded, one student after another—each one a male—got up to close a window. Finally, at about 8:15 a.m., a student stood up and closed the last open window in the room." At that point, the alumnus said, the professor suddenly stopped his lecture. Moving away from the podium, he spoke extemporaneously and forcefully to the class.

"You see, *you can't take it*," he said. "You wear all these clothes that college students find trendy. They're made out of inferior materials—and they're overpriced. And they don't keep out the cold." The professor then showed the lining of his coat jacket. "I bought this suit eight years ago at [he named a men's shop in Newport News]. It's fully lined. It's all wool. It contains no synthetic material, except in the lining. *This suit was made to last.*" He then raised one trousered

leg after another. "Now these shoes that I'm wearing today," he said, "they're about the same age as the suit. They're what I would call 'hefty shoes,' *built to last.* You wear them on a cold day, and you find that your feet remain warm. Why? Because the shoes are made entirely of leather. And leather is a poor conductor of cold."

"Now," the professor continued, "I could have taught this entire fifty-minute class with every window wide open. It wouldn't have bothered me *one bit*. As for you students, you should learn to look at clothes and life for *serviceability*, and not for mere fashion."

The alumnus finished his recollection. "He kept me interested every day," he said. "There was something new in every class. He had definite views. He was going to express them. And when I look back, I see that most of them were right."

28. An Anomaly for Her Era

The first theater in the American colonies was built in Williamsburg in 1716, so it is surprising that it required until 1926—210 years—for William & Mary to establish a drama program in Williamsburg. But schools or departments dedicated to the performing arts were slow to form in most of the United States. What is perhaps more surprising is that the founder and first director of William & Mary's theater department was a woman.

In 1926, fourteen members—26 percent of the William & Mary teaching faculty—were women. Two of the women held the rank of professor, two associate professor, and three assistant professor, while seven were instructors. Most of these women faculty were assigned to four departments—Modern Language, Physical Education, Secretarial Science, and Home Economics. By vote of the faculty, William & Mary phased out the last two departments in the 1960s.

Prior to the social changes of the 1960s and 1970s, colleges and universities usually chose male over female candidates for faculty positions. But the woman who became the founding director of undergraduate theater at William & Mary was an anomaly. As an undergraduate at Allegheny College, she had displayed a passion for theater and the performing arts. After graduating, she had studied drama at the University of Michigan, at Columbia University, and at Harvard. In later years she always identified herself as coming from Boston.

In thirty-one active years on the faculty, she made William & Mary nationally known for theater. She influenced virtually every student who came through the program. Even after her retirement, she attended most performances put on by the theater. She, along with the colorful figure she trained to succeed her, helped launch the careers of five decades of actors on Broadway and in Hollywood. Twenty years after the professor came to William & Mary, Colonial Williamsburg began its long-running outdoor summer drama, *The Common Glory*. It depicted the birth of a nation. She became its first director. When the original Phi Beta Kappa Hall and its stage burned in 1953, she provided (in a colleague's description) "the passion, vision, and drive" behind the construction of a new Phi Beta Kappa Memorial Hall. By her death in 1971, she was significant enough in the field of drama that the *New York Times* printed her obituary.

"She was an anomaly for her era," explained a William & Mary senior who wrote an honors thesis on the theater professor. "During an era when marriage and motherhood were expected of upper-middle-class women, she was a single, female professor who never married and had no children. In her professional world, she was always in the minority. Her educational experiences with other women, however, created a comfortable environment." As the honors thesis declared, she was "able to thrive and perform confidently."

During the three decades she taught at William & Mary, neither affirmative action nor the upward trajectory of some women in

theater and film had yet begun. Nevertheless, this theater professor, this professional, was a feminist whose work preceded her era.

29. A Gatekeeper for Precision

Raised during the Depression in a small Virginia town, the student graduated from William & Mary with a degree in chemistry. He took graduate degrees in chemistry at the University of Michigan and the University of Virginia. After receiving the PhD, he joined the chemistry faculty at William & Mary in 1945.

In the 1950s and 1960s, members of his department were able to do little publishing. Their teaching load was large, and most were devoted to top-quality teaching. As a result, little time remained for their personal research in the laboratory. The professor shared the same commitment to teaching, but during his first few years at William & Mary, he published an article in a leading chemistry journal—at the time, a major achievement. When his research appeared in print, the department chair asked him to come to his office for a talk.

When the young professor was seated, the chair tossed a copy of the scholarly journal on the desk. "Is this your article?" the chair asked. The new professor proudly said it was. Whereupon the chair said, "Well, if you have this kind of time on your hands, perhaps I should assign you another class to teach." To his credit, the chair was undoubtedly thinking of the reduction of class size that would result if the new faculty member taught one more course each semester. But the story was passed down for years among members of the Department of Chemistry as an indication of how out of fashion it then was in their department to publish research.

In the 1960s, William & Mary's small chemistry department started to change. It began to attract faculty who graduated from prestigious PhD programs. Its members began to receive national grants for research, with some faculty invited to hold visiting positions at world-class institutions. Competing with top international chemists, members of its faculty won scholarly awards. The Department of Chemistry became nationally known not only for teaching but also for research. Year after year the department ranked in the top ten chemistry departments in the nation in the number of majors it graduated annually. Every year, William & Mary produced the largest number of medical students of any Virginia college or university. In his later years, the professor himself published a textbook on inorganic chemistry. Active in Phi Beta Kappa, he was the Alpha chapter's recording secretary for twenty-five years.

"He was extremely precise and insisted on precision in the lab from his students," recounts a chemistry major who graduated from William & Mary in the 1950s, went on to the Yale School of Medicine, and became a noted cancer researcher. The alumnus also characterized the professor as "a gatekeeper for would-be chemistry majors and medical school applicants." He explained, "Not having done well in his course, some changed their career direction. Others were encouraged and came to believe that if they did well in his course, their other goals were indeed possible."

The professor's colleagues saw his unconventional side. "He did not care for windows in offices or for chewing gum or for listening to the radio," a former chair of chemistry remembers. "He was an avid NASCAR fan. Among students, he became infamous for his careful records of pipette calibrations."

But another faculty member recalls, "Any student who enrolled in his courses learned a great deal. He was very intelligent. He never forgot anything he ever learned or experienced."

Like others who had lived through the Great Depression, the professor embraced frugality. He would raid the campus dumpsters

for discarded paper and old glassware, for example, and put them back into use. He sent numerous memos about campus procedures to the dean. One year the dean asked, "We're old friends. Why do you *always* beat me up?" The chemistry professor responded, "Because it's my only fringe benefit."

30. Greater Gaiety: Coming Out at William & Mary

A William & Mary faculty member hired in the 1980s was discreetly gay. He kept his orientation quiet because he wanted, in his words, to "earn my appointment without either invisible tugs of solidarity or disapproval from some members of the search committee." One senior professor humorously suggested that William & Mary had hired him "because southern colleges still felt flattered when they landed northern faculty." After joining the faculty, he found that no one on campus mentioned his sexual orientation, though some found oblique ways to comment on his difference. As the years went on, his commitment to medieval studies, his frank and comfortable Roman Catholicism, and a midwestern breeziness were what defined him to colleagues.

Before the new professor came to Williamsburg, he had long been involved in campus ministry. At William & Mary, he soon started a Gay Student Support Group (the GSSG) that met every Monday night when school was in session and ran for twenty-four years. Gathering in a Williamsburg church basement coincidentally named "the Catacombs," the group hosted hundreds of earnest undergraduates over the decades. At these meetings, gay students were introduced to each other, related their personal stories, and came out to themselves. Some attended only a few sessions and moved on. Others kept coming. In this circle of trusted peers, they felt accepted and safe.

Partnering at first with local clergy as well as with the Student Health Center and Psychological Services, the GSSG acquiesced to the cautious silence of the university administration on matters of sexual orientation. The GSSG also endured the denunciations of parishioners who learned about the group's existence and its meetings in their church's buildings. One night, the gay faculty advisor arrived to start the meeting and found the building surrounded by police cars. The parish had received a bomb threat.

The 1980s and 1990s were the age of AIDS. Within the Gay Student Support Group, as well as elsewhere on the William & Mary campus, the gay faculty organizer served as a conduit for information on safe-sex practices for gay and heterosexual students. Misinformation fueled fear. Some believed that gay men "caused" AIDS, that all gays and lesbians were promiscuous, or that any gay male who fell ill must have been infected with HIV. When a gay professor died of cancer, rumors swirled that—all evidence to the contrary—it must have been AIDS. Alumni and students acquired an increasingly political edge, contributing sewn memorial panels for the NAMES Project (AIDS Quilt) and marching with a William & Mary banner in the 1987 gay-rights March on Washington. There was reason to feel on edge. The murder of Matthew Shepard in 1998 was preceded by deadly local attacks on lesbian couples along the Appalachian Trail in 1988 and among the Colonial Parkway murders in 1986. The belief among the sexually active straight community that it would not be affected by AIDS created a delusion of safety. As a result, national STD infection rates rose sharply. At William & Mary, as at other schools, faculty and students who were infected with HIV silently withdrew to die unseen off campus. Few university communities learned of these deaths and almost never got to mourn them.

The same faculty member served as the local anchor when gay William & Mary alumni decided to form their own caucus and host independent events during homecoming. The University Advancement Office informed the group that they could not donate under the name of William & Mary Gay and Lesbian Alumni or GALA, so the alums asked Swem Library if they could endow an acquisitions account for gender studies. The head librarian gladly welcomed them. When the endowment, named in honor of Richard Cornish—the first person executed for a charge of sodomy in the American colonies—was established in 1993, thousands of dollars poured in. Alumni who had previously never donated to William & Mary contributed. A decade had to pass before the university's Advancement Office found a way to recognize the gay group by name. It also began to solicit contributions from members of the gay support group. As of 2020, a discreet in-house list of sympathetic alumni donors has grown to nearly two-thousand names.

Attitudes toward gays and lesbians on campus quickly evolved in the 1990s. Outspoken faculty and staff emerged in growing numbers as allies. At the same time, everyone worked under the threat of backlash from traditionalist and conservative forces within the Board of Visitors and Virginia's legislature. As the decade progressed, benefits for the partners of gay and lesbian employees became a prominent recruitment and retention issue in higher education. Among public universities, the University of Iowa led the way in recognizing gay and lesbian partnerships in 1992. In 1993, Harvard University became the first private university to offer same-sex partner benefits to its employees. More quickly than expected, whole state university systems such as those in New York followed the lead of vanguard institutions. So did high-tech companies, large financial services corporations, and even the Big Three automakers.

At William & Mary, the same openly gay faculty member launched a campaign for equal employment benefits. He was joined by over a dozen other faculty and staff who for the most part still kept their sexual

orientation off the public record. William & Mary was something of an epicenter for a Virginia-wide conversation on the question of benefits for domestic partners. Senior administrators were caught between their personal sympathies and defending the university from political reprisals. One powerful state legislator from a rural county warned every president of a college or university in the Virginia system that their budgets would be cut if they publicly supported gay rights.

To the frustration of gays and lesbians and their supporters, Virginia continued to lag in national and even international trends. This political logjam lingered until 2015, when the US Supreme Court (by a vote of 5–4) declared same-sex marriages the equal of opposite-sex unions. The watershed case *Obergefell v. Hodges* extended the basic right to marry to same-sex couples through the Fourteenth Amendment.

Societal change eventually worked what legislation and mounting currents of goodwill from older generations could not. Freshmen arrived at William & Mary in the 1990s and early 2000s already firmly self-identified as LGBTQ, ready to live their sexual orientation openly in college. Student Affairs at William & Mary instituted an expanded nondiscrimination policy and formally recognized student-run LGBTQ clubs and advocacy groups. Well before the gay faculty member who had guided the movement on campus had retired in 2016, the era of gay people meeting in secret had long been discarded in myth and practice.

31. An Academically Indifferent Goof-Off

At least one professor at William & Mary never forgot where he came from academically. As the years went on, he wanted to remember that he was very much in background what he termed "an academically indifferent goof-off." Like most professors, he talked little about his personal life in class. But one year he happened to mention during a lecture the reason he had entered the profession of college teaching. To his surprise, at least a half-dozen students from the class dropped by his office in the following week to talk about what he had said.

The professor now realized that college students needed to hear more during college about how people decide what to do with their lives. He began to include a two-minute sketch in his classes about his background as "an academically indifferent goof-off." Over the years he gradually added details—about how he should have started college at twenty-one at the earliest, how he should have taken the great professors at his university even if the courses were difficult, how he should have learned at least one foreign language well, etc. The brief reminiscences gradually became a longer story. Finally he stopped giving the lecture in every class and instead gave it as a biannual lecture in the William & Mary Lecture Series. Taken from the now-retired professor's notes, the final version of that lecture reads:

I was an academic goof-off in college. I aimed at just getting by. And I did; I did just enough to get by. As a result, I wasted most of college.

But in the period of torpor that masqueraded as junior year, I was spending one semester at Wayne State University in Detroit, where my father was a longtime administrator. I should add that he was a nervous administrator that semester, for he feared I was going to embarrass him and flunk all of my courses. And that, of course, was a definite possibility.

I declared a major in English. By happenstance the courses required for that degree included one titled "American English." This course in linguistic history was taught by an unpretentious middle-aged professor. He looked very much like what students at the time called a "square." He sat at his desk to lecture, read his notes, and included a series of corny jokes based on the history of the English language. Even though he had surely told the same jokes many times, he still found them infinitely humorous. Almost alone in the class, he laughed—no, cackled—*at their end. If I had not needed the course for credit, I would have dropped it very quickly.*

And then, unexpectedly, in the third week of the semester, things began to change. I began to become interested, even fascinated, by the material covered in class and in reading. That semester I was living at home. After dinner one night, I told my father that I especially liked one course at his university. I named it and gave him the name of the professor. My father's bearing immediately changed. He focused his full attention on me. In a tone of great respect, he said the professor's full name and then said, "He's a scholar *... a* scholar.*"*

My father had advised me previously to take college seriously; I had not listened—for I thought college was for fun. This time the near awe in his tone caught my attention. I replied, "A 'scholar' ... is that good?*" My father then extolled the scholarly life as he—a university administrator—had observed it over the years. He stressed the quest for truth that was at the heart of scholarship.*

I ended up becoming a professor and a scholar. But I warn you: When you have been a known goof-off, it is difficult to convince graduate admission committees that you are now serious about academics. The doors to prestigious schools are simply hard for goof-offs to open. Admission committees are not being cruel or unforgiving when they turn down reformed goof-offs; they simply have too many applications from students who have rarely received less than an A in sixteen years of education. Goof-offs dig academic holes so deep they are difficult to climb out of. To be sure, if you persist, it may work out. A decade after taking that class in linguistic history and after military service, divinity school, and graduate school, I taught my first college course.

In life it is crucial that we thank people who have helped us. I had always planned to write the Wayne State professor who taught that course. But I never did, for something always seemed to intervene. But when I went on my first leave from William & Mary, I found to my relief that the professor—now in his eighties—was still alive. I quickly sat down and wrote a letter to him expressing my gratitude. It described my earlier indifference toward learning, my absorption in the materials of his class, and the concern for scholarship his teaching had aroused. I told him that he reminded me of Chaucer's famous clerk: "Gladly would he learn, and gladly teach." In a week I received a handwritten reply from an address in a western state. Among other things, the retired professor's letter said something like, "I wish I could come to see you. We could have a long talk. But I do not drive anymore. My wife and I moved out here to be near our daughter, where she can keep an eye on us." I was touched by his reply.

Every year the William & Mary professor concluded this public lecture by asserting that all colleges and universities have courses and faculty who can lead students "to the light." And every year his account caused students to visit his office to discuss their future.

32. A Civilizing Force

Whenever the government professor lost interest during an interview with a job candidate, she would decide that the conference room was too warm. She would walk over and open a window. Whether she knew it or not, her colleagues in the department interpreted those actions—which one described as "the opposite of white smoke emerging from the Vatican"—to mean that this applicant would not gain her vote.

Raised close to the Vermont border in upstate New York, the professor came from an old, established family that took education seriously. Her brother graduated from Yale University and Harvard Business School. She attended the University of Michigan and received her MA and PhD degrees from Columbia University. After Columbia she worked for some years in the Department of State. In Washington and later in Williamsburg, she became a genuine expert in French politics and well versed in British politics. She spoke so little about her work in Washington during World War II that rumors had it that she was assigned to a covert organization.

Learning in 1953 of a teaching opening in her field at William & Mary, she applied. Given Williamsburg's proximity to Washington DC, the position must have been attractive. But at that time, few of William & Mary's faculty were women. In 1953 most applicants for such a position would have been males in their late twenties, fresh from graduate school. She was also older than the typical candidate. Traditionally, a department would prefer to hire a younger professor—one who would remain active for a longer time before retiring. Most of the time, that professor would be a male. Nevertheless, William & Mary hired her in 1953. Her assigned title of "acting assistant professor" may reflect the department's mixed approval of a candidate who was not only female but also older. But as the years went on, she was promoted, and her title lost its "acting" qualifier. At William & Mary, she became what faculty and students recognized as a "civilizing force" in their lives. "She was one of the people who made undergraduate education special," William & Mary's twenty-fifth president, a former student, declared. Eventually she became a full professor and department chair. "She commanded a lot of respect," a woman professor recalled.

While at William & Mary, she specialized in comparative politics and international relations. At the same time, she also taught courses on American government and other topics. She led seminars in France and published several important articles on British and French politics. "She was passionate about everything French," a colleague remembered. On occasions when her senior seminar met at her home in Williamsburg, she introduced her students to the finest French cheese and red wine.

When serving as chair of government, she was strict. If members of her department were late to office hours, she called their homes. If a professor was chronically late, she put a copy of his or her contract into the tardy professor's mailbox. "Prim and proper" was how many of her colleagues viewed her. "She was eccentric but very kind," a physics professor remembered. Another colleague commented, "She would break the clutch on her new cars two weeks into ownership—and then describe her broken cars as 'lemons.'"

In the classroom, she held high standards and well-defined views of what she liked and did not like. She could become angry if a student was unprepared or lazy. But she spent an enormous amount of time helping undergraduates with their writing and honors theses. Diligent students were struck by her kindness and generosity. "She was so kind to me," a former advisee remembers. "She helped me realize that I could be more than I thought academically." A half century later, that student—a future vice president for student affairs—ended up having a building on William & Mary's campus named after him.

The women's movement came to William & Mary in the 1970s. "It *tiptoed* in," a senior administrator from that time commented, "and with only a few exceptions was firmly repulsed." In the 1960s and '70s, a series of laws passed by Congress and executive orders issued by presidents prohibited gender discrimination in areas ranging from employment to housing. In 1975 the first American research university appointed a woman as president.

A younger member of the faculty remembers being invited in the 1970s to talk on the Equal Rights Amendment to one of the professor's classes. "I have a memory of a spirited conversation with the class and of my being pretty assertive," the professor recalls. "Afterwards she said something to the effect that she admired my outspokenness and wished she could be more like that." Although younger female faculty took the reins of the women's movement at William & Mary, their elder colleague in government remained supportive of the movement from afar. The same faculty member observed, "[She] showed a consciousness that might not have been typical of her generation."

In 1986, her thirty-third year at William & Mary, she had a stroke. Taken to a hospital in Newport News, she remained in a deep coma.

Friends from the faculty—especially spouses of her male colleagues—paid frequent visits. In the hospital, routine paperwork revealed that she was born in 1914—not in 1924, as her William & Mary file showed. She died in 1993. In her will, she left a generous monetary gift to establish professorships for the purpose of augmenting faculty salaries. From childhood on, William & Mary's first female government professor was the kind of person whose honesty was never questioned. Yet, during a time when women found it difficult to have a career in academia, she took ten years off her age to improve her chance of being hired. It is difficult to fault her.

33. Sneakers

For some years, the creative writing courses at William & Mary were taught by a graduate of one of the most renowned writing workshops in the nation. For William & Mary faculty, with their heavy teaching loads, he was well published, even appearing in the *New Yorker*. He was also a published poet. A bachelor, the storied professor owned a Welsh corgi named Sneakers. Everybody knew Sneakers. William & Mary's campus contains small outbuildings patterned on their eighteenth-century counterparts and assigned as coveted offices to members of the English faculty. The creative writing professor had his office in one.

One evening, when the professor left his office to walk home, he found he had locked not only his keys but also Sneakers inside

the outbuilding. In that era before cell phones, the professor finally found a phone on campus and called a slender member of his department for help. The chances were good, he thought, that his colleague might be able to climb into the outbuilding through its one window. When the thin colleague arrived, he climbed halfway into the building through its eighteenth-century replica window but then became firmly stuck.

After a long time, he succeeded in getting unstuck and into the outbuilding and unlocking the door. There was both rejoicing and relief. Sneakers was reunited with his master, and everyone could finally go home. But this wasn't the first—or the last—time that Sneakers was hampered by human error.

The professor's house was a ten-minute walk away from campus. Its living room was on the second floor. The back door on the second floor opened to a back porch, from which a set of steps led to the ground. One night, during a faculty party, Sneakers wanted to go outside. The professor opened the door to the back porch, Sneakers' usual route to the yard. Too late, the professor remembered that a workman had removed the floor of the back porch earlier that day.

Sneakers happily pranced out, anticipating the joys that awaited a dog in a backyard. And then his perspective changed. His little legs began to pedal furiously, searching for the missing floorboards of the porch. He *knew* they were there *somewhere*. Still trying all the way down to find a foothold, he plummeted to the ground.

The guests at the party rushed downstairs. They found the dog unharmed but stunned and unmoving. One guest suggested that Sneakers was saying to himself over and over, "To err is human ... but to forgive ... is canine."

34. Liquor by the Drink

A certain science professor enjoyed going out for a cocktail or a drink, in the parlance of the time. Until recent years, no restaurants in Williamsburg or surrounding James City County served mixed drinks or what was called "liquor by the drink." Residents or visitors to Williamsburg could buy package liquor from state stores, but to have a cocktail they needed to go to a different county or town. That Williamsburg was "dry" inevitably affected the economy. Couples would come to Williamsburg for a long weekend, go to a quietly elegant Colonial Williamsburg restaurant for dinner, and be told by the waitperson that the only martini the bar could legally serve had to be made with wine.

Taverns and drinking have been regulated in Virginia as far back as the seventeenth century. By the twentieth century, the commonwealth had experienced numerous temperance movements and efforts to control alcohol consumption, especially "hard" or "distilled" liquor. In 1968, the citizens of Virginia voted to allow sales of "liquor by the drink," but only in restaurants and only up to a certain percentage of total sales. Periodically, counties across the state could vote on liquor by the drink. Those counties that voted for it were classified as "wet"; counties that voted against it became "dry." Like students at most colleges and universities, William & Mary students did drink alcohol. And so did many faculty. Theoretically, liquor was not permitted in offices, dormitories, or fraternity or sorority housing. But on Sunday mornings, empty beer cans overflowed the trash cans and dumpsters adjacent to the fraternity lodges.

Until the 1970s, at least one illegal speakeasy operated in James City County, and the science professor occasionally patronized it. But a person could legally get a mixed drink in Williamsburg and the surrounding area in two places. The first was a private bottle club located in the basement of the Williamsburg Inn. Members could keep liquor and wine in rented lockers. A second, lesser-known place was a miniature golf course. Located in a part of Williamsburg that technically belonged to adjacent York County, a "wet" county, the golf course became a drinking spot for a few of the older faculty and their friends. They drank while tourists and their children played miniature golf.

In addition, the historic town of Yorktown, 13 miles from Williamsburg on the scenic Colonial Parkway, contained several bars that served not only food but also alcohol. One restaurant, the Wharf, which extended over the York River, became a favorite gathering place for younger people. One of its steady customers was the unmarried science professor. To have a few nighttime drinks, he often drove the 13 miles between towns. On one such Friday night at the Wharf, the scientist asked a new member of the faculty if he wanted to have a final drink in Williamsburg. The new faculty member had heard that the young professor's house was decorated with considerable originality, and he accepted the invitation and followed him home.

Because of the alcohol he had consumed, the professor drove back to Williamsburg at 15 miles per hour. Although police view driving well below the speed limit as a possible sign of drunk driving, the professor believed he could drive safely and not draw attention if he stayed at that speed. The slow pace frustrated the new instructor enormously. Several times during the drive he depressed his gas pedal, pulled up to the side of the science professor, and gestured by tapping his watch and making a "hurry-up" motion. But each time the professor continued to look straight ahead and to creep along at 15 miles per hour. Bicyclists pedaled faster. The young instructor consumed cigarette after cigarette on the journey. When he had finished one, he would jab the stub in his ashtray and immediately light another.

Sixty minutes after leaving the Wharf, the two William & Mary faculty members arrived at their destination on a residential street. When the new faculty member sat down in the professor's living room, he immediately noticed that the focus of the room was a large animal hide rug, bearing the pattern of a symmetrical saddle. When the instructor asked what animal that hide had been taken from, the science professor replied, "*Guess.*" It was an easy question to answer, but the instructor was not a zoologist. He pondered the question and looked at the rug from several angles. Finally, he confessed that the identification was on the tip of his tongue, but that ultimately he could not identify the hide. Clearly savoring the moment (as he surely had done on many previous occasions), the professor leaned back in his chair and said, "*That is a cow.*"

As tourism grew and times changed, liquor in all forms became more available in Virginia's colonial capital. The bottle club closed; the speakeasy disappeared. Today, mixed drinks are served in many establishments within walking distance of the campus of William & Mary. To get a drink, professors need not haunt a speakeasy or drive 13 miles out of town.

35. Women in a STEM World

As late as 1983, the American Association of University Professors acknowledged in their *Administrative Issues Journal* that few women served on college or university faculties.[1] This assertion was especially true in the fields of science, technology, engineering, and mathematics (STEM). But as early as the 1960s, William & Mary's biology department had three women professors, two of whom were nationally known. This vignette names them because they were well known in their time and are now deceased.

The esteemed botanist Bernice Speece was a William & Mary graduate. While an undergraduate, Speece began doing research under the direction of professor J. T. Baldwin, an award-winning plant geneticist. Baldwin joined the faculty in the 1938–1939 school year. When he left in 1939, she continued to research under the direction of the department chair, a plant geneticist. When she submitted an academic paper on her research to the *American Journal of Botany*, they accepted it. The chair was so impressed that he arranged for Speece to submit her completed work to the biology faculty in the form of a master's thesis, even though the department lacked a graduate program. Both the William & Mary's administrators and its Board of Visitors agreed with the recommendation. In 1941, the degree was granted. She became the first person (and first woman) to receive a graduate degree in biology from William & Mary.

Armed with a master's degree, Speece went to the University of Virginia and earned a PhD in biology. In 1946, the department chair invited her to join William & Mary's faculty. He also persuaded Baldwin to return to the biology department. Baldwin and Speece began a decades-long research collaboration. Baldwin considered her better at preparing plant cells for chromosomal examination than anyone he had encountered in his career. During a thirty-year career, Speece authored or coauthored more than thirty scientific papers. She taught courses in genetics and cytogenetics. In addition, she served as the organizer and coordinator for William & Mary's large introductory biology course. Retiring as an associate professor in 1976, she died in 1985.

A second member of the biology faculty, Charlotte Magnum, specialized in comparative invertebrate physiology. Prior to coming to Williamsburg, she took a BS at Vassar College in the interesting combination of philosophy and zoology. This background may explain why she was also a published poet. In the words of one obituary, Professor Magnum "saw beauty, as well as biochemistry, in the blue crab and all creatures." She earned an MS in zoology and a PhD in biology from Yale University. After postdoctoral study at the University of London, she joined the William & Mary faculty in 1964.

In thirty-two years at William & Mary, Professor Magnum achieved excellence not only in scholarship but also in teaching. For someone with the high teaching load of a William & Mary professor in her era, her scholarly output was incredible. She wrote 150 articles on biology for many different scientific journals. In addition, she edited several books and served on twelve editorial boards. She held visiting teaching or research positions at universities in Denmark, Louisiana, and California. Her honors included the presidency of the American Society of Zoologists, the Lifetime Achievement Award in Research of the Crustacean Society, and the first Dean's Award at William & Mary for Scholarship in the Arts & Sciences.

Magnum held high standards in teaching and research. She was known as a "tough grader," impatient with students who made no attempt to reach the same high standards. She expected students to reflect excellence. As her sister declared, teaching was even more important to her than research. If obliged to choose between the classroom and the laboratory, she would clearly have chosen the classroom. "She influenced many students," her sister concluded, "and they adored her." In 1996, Magnum retired as the Chancellor Professor of Biology. She died from cancer in 1998. Shortly before her death, she told her sister, "You know, I've been happy every day of my life, doing what I do."

Magnum had a profound effect on those she taught. A year before her death, twenty-four of her former students, known by biologists throughout the United States as "Charlotte's Students," presented a symposium of their research at William & Mary to honor her. Following her death, the biology faculty established an annual prize in her name, awarded to the outstanding research student among graduating biology majors.

The contributions of a female microbiologist, Grace Blank, have tended to be overshadowed by those of Speece and Magnum. But Blank also left a lasting impression in the department. When the biology department was in Millington Hall, a large portrait of Blank hung on the wall, and the microbiology lab was formally named the Grace J. Blank Microbiology Laboratory. Her portrait was moved to the microbiology laboratory in the new Integrated Science Center when Millington Hall was replaced. In a departmental tradition, her metal typing table, with her name written underneath in her handwriting, is passed down to the newest full professor of microbiology. Professor Blank left much of her estate to the university. Her will stated that all funds from the endowment must be used to support an annual award for the outstanding teaching of microbiology.

Ever since the Russian launch of Sputnik, American leaders have worried about falling behind other countries in science and technology. Today, the low percentage of students entering these fields continues to be a concern. In 2001, the National Science Foundation coined the acronym STEM. Various STEM curriculums are at the forefront of education designed to prepare a capable workforce. Several of the programs are focused on efforts to attract more females to the STEM fields. While paralleled elsewhere at a few colleges and universities, the presence of such outstanding women science faculty was rare for its time.

III. ALUMNI AND LIFE AFTER WILLIAM & MARY

36. The National Transportation Award

One weekday morning, an architectural historian on the faculty received a telephone call from the vice president for development. Could he possibly drive an alumnus from the Class of 1926 to Virginia's Brunswick County on Saturday? Located adjacent to North Carolina, rural Brunswick County once had many plantations.

The alumnus was the last living member of a leading (or "first") family of Virginia (FFV). A bachelor, he had lived in Santa Fe since serving in World War II. He rarely visited his native South but was currently staying on campus in the president's guesthouse. The purpose of his visit was to discuss whether to bequeath his estate to William & Mary.

The FFV descendant had expressed a strong desire to visit his ancestral home in Brunswick County one last time. Since he had mentioned it three times, the president and vice president for development decided that William & Mary should make such a visit possible. The alumnus did not have a car.

"My kids play soccer on Saturdays," the professor replied to the vice president's request.

"Yes," said the vice president. "But you do teach the college's course on Virginia architecture. Could you possibly—possibly—arrange to drive to Brunswick County? Just this one Saturday? Our alumnus's undergraduate years have clearly begun to mean more and more to him. At his age, he needs to be fussed over a bit. The president really would like to accommodate him."

The professor was quiet for a minute. "Well," he finally said, reluctantly, "I guess I could. My wife can take the kids to soccer."

"Wonderful, wonderful. Thank you," the vice president said. He continued: "You should know that he is a little eccentric. He served in combat in World War II and rose to be a captain—with many medals. But he talks nonstop. About World War II. About dogs. Or if he doesn't talk about those subjects, he talks about his family. He'll talk you to death.

"And one more thing," the vice president concluded. "The president and I consider this a high-stress assignment. He has the potential to drive you crazy. Please hang in there; we'll all be in your debt."

At nine o'clock on Saturday morning, the architectural historian was on the road with the elderly alumnus seated beside him. Lean,

exacting, persnickety, with the hint of a British accent picked up somewhere, he was nattily dressed in a blue blazer with a yacht club logo. Upon entering the professor's car, he immediately started talking. By James City County, he was talking about the invasion of France. By Prince George Courthouse, he was talking about the invasion of Germany. By Stony Creek, he had switched to the old Virginia families. When the two stopped at a roadside restaurant in Jarratt for lunch, the professor hoped he could dine in peace. But his passenger talked about dogs through-out the meal. He owned four—all with distinct personalities, each of which he described in detail.

When the car finally reached the eighteenth-century family estate—a Georgian Revival mansion—the current owners came out to greet them. The alumnus declined their invitation to come into the house—"too emotionally wrenching," he told them, then repeated, "too emotionally wrenching." He walked around the grounds with the owners and the professor for forty-five minutes, talking nonstop. On the return drive to Williamsburg, the alumnus continued to talk, mostly adding details to his earlier stories. When the professor dropped him off at the president's guesthouse, it was 5:10 p.m. Instead of going home, the architectural historian went directly to his faculty office. He sat down at his typewriter and wrote the following memo to the vice president for development: "At nine a.m. today I picked up an alumnus from the Class of 1926 at the president's guesthouse. I drove him 119 miles to his family estate in Brunswick County. We walked around the estate for forty-five minutes. I then drove our alumnus back to the president's guesthouse and arrived at five-ten p.m." He ended the statement with "Respectfully submitted," signed his name, sealed the envelope, and put it in the interdepartmental mailbox.

Two weeks later, the professor found in his mailbox a typed and framed document bearing a handsome gold seal. The document read:

NATIONAL TRANSPORTATION AWARD

to
[here the professor's name appeared]
for
sacrifice in the service
of fund raising
beyond—well beyond—the call of duty.

It was signed by the vice president for development. The alumnus died two years after his visit. The professor who drove him to Brunswick County is now retired, but the framed National Transportation Award hangs on the wall of his home office. And, yes, the alumnus left his estate to William & Mary.

37. The Boring Occupation

She was a leader in her high school class, was an outstanding student, and was elected to two honorary societies in college. During her four years at William & Mary, she was involved in theater, landing a major role as an entering freshman. She was active in music and also in Greek life. She was an excellent literary critic; her English professors considered her one of the best students in their classes. One of her professors, after reading a paper she had written for his class, insisted that she apply to graduate school. In sum, she was the kind of student whom graduating classes across the nation would vote "most likely to succeed."

But after graduating from William & Mary, attending graduate school, marrying, and beginning a promising career at a university, she opted to take a job in Washington. The decision surprised her friends. Her descriptions to friends of her work seemed to indicate that she spent a lot of time in administration. Over the years, she gained several promotions but seemed to remain in essentially the same job. Whenever friends asked if she were going to leave that position and move to another one, she replied that, unlike many people, she *enjoyed* her job. She was in no hurry to leave for another one. After a half dozen or so years working, she seemed so content in her career that her friends stopped wringing their hands behind her back. William & Mary professors with whom she had kept in touch ceased lamenting her lack of ambition.

And then she retired. And this was Washington, DC. She had not worked in administration at all. She was CIA.

38. From Dinwiddie County to Harvard

The student from Southside Virginia spent first grade in a segregated community school in a rural county in Virginia. He spent the second and third grades in a segregated elementary school 25 miles from his family's home. When the county schools were integrated, he was in the fourth grade. He continued to attend the same elementary school, but— under integration—it had a new name. The student's mother impressed on him the importance of education. From his freshman year in a county high school onward, he played football, was elected team captain, and was later named all-district defensive end. During his junior and senior years, he drove a school bus and worked part-time at a local supermarket. Despite his part-time jobs and commitments to athletics, he graduated high in his class.

Following graduation, the student, then eighteen years old, worked full-time at a supermarket and part-time at a construction job. He now had a wife and child to provide for. He left the supermarket and took a position in Richmond as a security officer for Virginia's largest utility. Many years later, when he applied for a promotion at the utility, the interviewer told him that he lacked "any formal education." Hearing the phrasing as an insult and wanting to show his son (now in high school) how important education was, he enrolled in a small junior college ten minutes from his house. It had an arrangement that permitted students with high grades and strong recommendations to transfer with junior standing to William & Mary.

During his first semester of junior college, the student was befriended by its president. "He was genuinely interested in my educational experience," the student remembers, "and [he] checked on my progress often, ... summoned me to his office on a number of occasions, [and] encouraged me to work on ... committees."

Once graduated from the junior college and accepted at William & Mary, the student began to commute 70 miles from his rural county to Williamsburg several days per week. He would leave at 6:30 in the morning and drive for ninety minutes. After classes, he would make another ninety-minute drive to begin his job at the utility by three o'clock in the afternoon. Following an eight-hour shift, he drove an hour to return home. On days when he attended classes, he spent four hours in Williamsburg, four hours on the road, and eight hours at his job. He made all of these drives in a 1986 pickup truck. When a professor once kidded him about his "rattletrap car," he politely answered that it was "actually a rattletrap *truck*."

One morning, a professor running an errand in Williamsburg saw the "rattletrap truck" waiting at an intersection for the light to change. It was then that the professor fully realized the extent of the student's commitment to education. By the time the "rattletrap truck" gave up the ghost that spring, it had reached 180,000 miles. It had also carried its owner to Marine Corps Reserve meetings, to active military duty two weekends a year, and to other obligations. He used what free time he had for academic matters and family obligations. "It was hard work," he reflected twenty years later, "and it required an abundance of time and sacrifice."

During the nontraditional student's two years at William & Mary, professors viewed him as a person of integrity, high intelligence, and great promise. Mature, organized, and affable, he came across as someone happy to be in college, regardless of the hardship connected with it. Since he rarely mentioned his long commute, few professors knew that he drove three hours to get to and from campus. A departmental secretary who was in a class with him described him as "my favorite student on campus."

A number of faculty offered advice and support. When one suggested remaining in college for a fifth year to take a master's degree in education, the student decided to do so. Another professor remembers their first talk in his office. "And where are you thinking of taking a master's degree in education?" the professor had asked. The student answered by naming a small state university in the Midwest. The professor was startled. He had grown up near that school. It was not particularly distinguished, and many people who lived outside the state had never heard of it.

"Well," the professor said after a pause, "I suspect it has some innovative programs. But let's look at some other options." He asked if the student had considered Indiana University. The student said he had not. The professor then told him about the prestigious reputation of its School of Education. The professor then named Harvard University, whose School of Education invariably ranked high in national surveys. The student was stunned. "Oh," he replied, "I could never get admitted there. Or afford it." The professor immediately replied, "Oh yes, you could, and you could get a scholarship that would *allow* you to afford it."

The student applied to the three master's programs. When Indiana University invited applicants to a weekend open house, he accepted the invitation, assuming a visit would give him a better sense of the school. After driving 673 miles, the student was talking at the reception with the faculty member in charge of the MEd program when she excused herself and went into her office. Through its glass windows, the student could see the professor making a series of short phone calls. Soon, he reported, other faculty started showing up. All came over to talk with him. Shortly after he returned to Virginia, an envelope from Indiana University containing a letter of acceptance and a full scholarship arrived at his home.

Harvard, however, had not yet sent its decision. The professor who had suggested applying to it feared that the student's application had been overlooked or misplaced.

The volume of applications the school's program received annually was overwhelming. Knowing that time was of the essence, he sent a copy of the recommendation he had written for the student to the assistant to the dean of the School of Education. He attached a separate note to it. If the dean's assistant found this recommendation significant, the professor's note asked, would she perhaps pass it on to the dean? Less than a week later, the student received an offer of a full scholarship to the prestigious school.

In the end, the student chose to attend Harvard University. Following two years there, he received the MEd degree. Returning home, he taught briefly at a liberal-arts, denominational college. This college was entering its last years following an economic slump. To keep the school afloat, its administration was steadily scuttling more faculty and staff than it was hiring. When he was cut from the faculty, the student secured the executive directorship of a community youth center and then taught social studies in a public high school. Later hired as an executive by the US Postal Service, he was steadily promoted and soon was managing government teams in Washington and serving as an advisor to postmasters general.

After a dinner that celebrated the student's most recent promotion, the wife of a William & Mary professor said with some concern to her husband, "You don't seem very happy about this promotion."

"Oh, I am, I am," said the professor. "He's doing great."

"Yes, he is. He's in charge of all mail to and from an entire continent, and more than that, you've always told me that people who attend seminars at 6 a.m. in Washington, DC, are very important people."

"Yes, they are. They are." After a moment he added, "But you don't understand."

"Understand *what*?"

"He should have been president of a college."

39. Always One Step Ahead

The student was raised in southwestern Virginia, a half hour away from West Virginia, Kentucky, and Tennessee, and almost as far west as Detroit. In the town of Lebanon, his mother was a high school guidance counselor, his grandfather had served in Virginia's House of Delegates, and his father was a lawyer who had also served as a circuit court judge. In the words of a newspaper story, he "bested everyone" in high school—valedictorian of his class, member of the National Honor Society, Eagle Scout. In athletics, he won all-region honors in football as well as varsity letters in wrestling and track. His classmates voted him "Most Likely to Succeed."

The family's relationship with William & Mary went back many decades, so as a high school senior, he applied to William & Mary as well as to Princeton University. Admitted to both, he chose William & Mary. He attended on a regional scholarship. It was named for a West Virginia senator and recognized "exceptionally able high school seniors who show promise of continued excellence." In four years in Williamsburg, he richly fulfilled that promise.

Every student at William & Mary takes a mandatory freshman seminar. The professor who taught the student's freshman seminar quickly realized that he had a student in class who would excel at any college anywhere. At a departmental meeting early in the semester, he told his colleagues, "History credits William & Mary with producing three presidents. Well, I may have the *fourth* in my freshman seminar this year." In the other courses the student took as a freshman, his professors tended to use the word "brilliant" to describe him. As college went on, writers of recommendations typically used such superlatives as "very mature," "very special," "very well adjusted," and even "very excellent" to describe him.

In his junior year, the student chose to major in chemistry. The chemistry professor who became his advisor and taught him in several classes later declared, "Even as an undergraduate, [he] always seemed one step ahead of everyone, including his own professor. In forty years as a professor of chemistry, he was one of the three best students I have taught."

Prior to graduating from William & Mary as a member of Phi Beta Kappa, he accepted admission to the PhD program in chemistry at Stanford University. It was one of the most highly competitive doctoral programs in chemistry in the nation. Four months after he graduated from William & Mary, the 9/11 terrorist attacks on New York City and Washington, DC, occurred. In the months following, the student continued his doctoral work somewhat reluctantly. Drawn to the military since childhood, he felt he should serve in America's war on terror. His father remembered that he was "livid" about the attack on the World Trade Center, "just furious that someone had attacked American citizens on our soil."

In graduate school at Stanford, as in undergraduate study at William & Mary, the student's professors viewed him as having a future on the cutting edge of science. "An exceptional person," his graduate mentor said, "a genuine friend." But two years after entering the PhD program at Stanford, he completed the master's degree and left graduate study.

Enlisting in the US Marines, he attended Officer Candidate School

(OCS) in Quantico, Virginia. Of the officer candidate schools in the US military, Quantico had the reputation of being the toughest. A professor who taught him commented, "I served as a lieutenant in the United States Army. But I never would have made it through Marine OCS. Too tough." Of the 220 members of his OCS class, the William & Mary student graduated first, as the honor graduate.

In the presidential elections of 2000 and 2004, he had voted for Democratic candidates. "My son told us, to our faces," his father remembered, "'I won't vote for Mr. Bush, but I'll take a bullet for him.'"

His father also remembered cautioning, "You realize you can be wounded in a way that can change your life, or you can lose your life."

His son had replied, "Dad, if I die, I did it doing my duty and protecting my country."

Commissioned upon graduation as a second lieutenant, the young officer was assigned to Iraq. Four months after arriving, he was killed in a firefight.

40. The Haunting Place

The 1971 graduate returned to live in Williamsburg. His return allowed him to reconnect with a favorite undergraduate professor. While a student, he enjoyed the professor's lecturing ability and courses. He wound up taking three of his classes. In addition to the professor's classroom skills, however, what made him a special person in the alumnus's view was that he stayed in touch after graduation.

Upon returning to Williamsburg, the former student worked for the Virginia Historic Landmark Commission, which then had an office on William & Mary's campus. While walking across campus one evening, he bumped into his favorite professor. The professor suggested they sit on a nearby bench and chat. That chat led to occasional lunches and dinners over the years, even to this day. Both men had a strong interest in American history and historical preservation.

Their lunches and dinners generally took place at the Downtown Shortstop Restaurant, located across Jamestown Road from Barksdale Field. Now gone but still lamented, the Downtown Shortstop was the kind of neighborhood establishment all colleges need adjacent to their campuses. After one dinner, the professor suggested a walk down Duke of Gloucester (DOG) Street to see something he described as "special." The two men walked to the Courthouse Green, stopping near the majestic live oak on the Green. They continued across Nicholson Street to the entrance of a long, narrow allée of tall boxwoods next to the historic St. George Tucker House. It was now dusk, and the student recalled not being able to see to the end of the allée.

The professor nonchalantly advised him to walk down the allée and promised to meet him at the other end. Alone, the student started down the narrow brick path of the allée, which was more like a tunnel of trees than a walkway. Even in the daylight, the tunnel was dark and mysterious. The combination of the twilight, the closed-in nature of the walkway, and the uncertainty of what awaited caused the student to feel more than a bit of nervous trepidation. He walked slowly, cautiously looking around with every step. More than once, the thought crossed his mind that this was some kind of fraternity initiation.

Upon reaching the end of the allée, he was greeted by the professor, who stood on an ivy-covered hillock topped with three live oaks and a wooden bench. The mount over-looked the Governor's Palace and adjacent grounds. Despite having lived in Williamsburg for a decade and having explored much of Colonial Williamsburg, the former student had never before discovered this particular place. It was such a haunting—in a good way—experience that it stayed with him through the years. As he subsequently learned, the allée is used in the initiation process of William & Mary's secret society, the Bishop Madison Society. Because of the society's connection, the allée is known as the Bishop Madison Grotto.

Sixteen years later, after a spring dinner in Merchant's Square with the woman he had been dating for three years, the alumnus suggested a leisurely stroll down DOG Street. When they arrived at the great oak, he asked the young woman to walk down the 30-yard allée, and they would, as the professor had said to him years before, meet at the other end. When they met, the former student escorted her up the steps to the top of the mount, where he asked her to marry him. She said yes.

A short six years later, his wife passed away. Since then, he has taken his two nieces to the allée and mount to show them where he proposed to their beloved aunt. They hugged and cried. To this day, he is not quite sure why the professor brought him there, but he was glad that he did. The grotto has been and ever will be a very special place for him.

IV. PRESIDENTS, PROVOSTS, AND DEANS

41. Speaking Styles of William & Mary Presidents

During the academic year, William & Mary, like many colleges, holds "convocations"—formal assemblies of administrators, faculty, and students led by the president. The fall convocation, which welcomes freshmen, is held on the lawn of the Wren Building. At these convocations, undergraduates sit in folding chairs, faculty "process" in academic regalia, a major public figure and the president speak, the choir sings, and freshmen are welcomed into the William & Mary community. Scheduled for the late afternoon and generally lasting an hour, the fall convocation is followed by a reception for the freshman class and a dinner on the Wren Lawn.

At one fall convocation in the 1990s, the guest speaker was a nationally known journalist and author. When the convocation concluded, the administrators, faculty, and student officers processed from the site and then dispersed. At the recession, two professors found themselves walking side by side. Speaking out of the side of his mouth (for it is bad form to talk in processions), one quietly said to the other,

"I wonder how much longer William & Mary can ethically invite leading figures to speak at its convocations, only to have them so thoroughly outspoken by its president." Also out of the side of his mouth, the other faculty member, an ethicist, replied with surprise, "I was just thinking the same thing."

The president is the principal representative of a college or university and its history and ideals. For virtually all presidents, being a good administrator, a wise financial manager, and a person of vision has been critical. In addition, it helps if the president is a good speaker. Presidents regularly speak to alumni about the needs of their alma mater. Presidents of state-supported schools regularly face the added challenge of persuading legislators that an institution is a worthy recipient of their financial support.

Presidents must also communicate their vision of education to students and faculty. In a sensitive and articulate way, they must explain to the public the inevitable crises and controversies of college life. Good speakers, especially if they gain parental support, tend to attract more donors and more and better applicants to a school.

Since 1693, William & Mary has had twenty-eight presidents. Seven have served since 1960. The achievements of college presidents can be contentious to discuss. The achievements and mistakes of many previous William & Mary presidents have long been known. A fresh approach would be to discuss how the speaking styles of these recent presidents reflected their presidencies. That is an especially appropriate approach for William & Mary, since most of its recent presidents have viewed their years in office as a *mission*. The following descriptions of their oratorical styles come from eight retired or active faculty who have heard them speak:

Former superintendent of public instruction for the commonwealth of Virginia and an alumnus, the twenty-second president of William & Mary served from 1960 to 1971. A native of a rural county in Virginia, he frequently mentioned early memories of plowing the fields of the family farm behind a mule. His speeches often quoted his father's advice: "Whatever you do in life, son, make sure you plow a straight furrow." Folksy, rural, southern, he filled his speeches with imagery, often referring to the campus as "sacred ground" and including such descriptions as looking at the Wren Building on a foggy evening and "seeing the ghosts of Jefferson, Monroe, and

Chief Justice John Marshall." One dean commented, "It was so easy to get distracted during his speeches by the imagery of the colonial-era heroes strolling across the Wren yard in the mist."

The twenty-third president of William & Mary, a Yale graduate, served from 1971 to 1985. A World War II veteran, he was educated in prestigious preparatory schools and universities. Slightly New England in manner, he was extremely respectful in what he said. In old New England style, he dropped his Rs frequently—*library*, for example, became *liberry*. Often focused on the goal of building community, his speeches were designed to nurture consensus; he did not aim at oratory. Listeners were drawn to what he said rather than to the way he said it. "William & Mary is on the edge of excellence," he declared in a speech early in his presidency. The words became a kind of defining phrase for his presidency.

The former dean of a southern law school and an alumnus, the twenty-fourth president served from 1985 to 1992. Logical, clear, concise, well organized, direct, and unadorned, his speeches avoided rhetorical flourishes. They were often confident and optimistic, but they could be blunt. On paper, his speeches were characterized by short sentences and the avoidance of qualifying clauses.

A dean of William & Mary's law school and an alumnus, the twenty-fifth president served from 1992 to 2005 and saw the new

century in. Homiletic, hortatory, headmasterly, and inspirational, his elegant speeches featured a graceful and often-poetic use of language and metaphor. When he spoke extemporaneously, his talks were often as good as his more carefully crafted formal speeches. Praising the president's meticulously prepared addresses, one faculty member recalls that they were "often elevated by citations of a wide range of intellectuals, both from the academy and without."

Which brings us back to the beginning of this vignette.

42. From a Forty-Seven-Year-Old Diary

Dear Diary:

9/26/72:

Had lunch at the soda fountain of what is called the Williamsburg Corner Drugstore. Found seated next to me an exotic and beautiful woman. Probably she, like me, was in her late twenties or early thirties.

*She looked like she had just walked off a fashion shoot—*Vogue *or* Cosmopolitan *or some such publication. Elegantly dressed, poised, she stood out boldly from us other eaters. As usual the lunchroom was crowded, but the seat at the counter beside her remained unoccupied through-out lunch. It seemed that nobody dared to actually sit next to her.*

My lectures go well in this new teaching position, Diary. The students understand my accent and I theirs. And they are a wonderful lot—intelligent, amusing, and outspoken.

9/30/72:

Saw "her" again. At the drug store again. And dared to sit next to her, if only briefly.

10/4/72:

And yet again. I encounter her on campus. This time I dared to follow her when she left. Surprisingly, she vanished into a college building called "the Brafferton." It's named, I'm told, for the Brafferton Manor in England. It supported William & Mary's Indian School during the colonial period. Now it houses the offices of the president and provost. At least, I think she disappeared into the Brafferton.

All I know is that she vanished shortly after crossing Duke of Gloucester Street into campus. Three buildings stand there—the Sir Christopher Wren Building, the President's House, and the Brafferton. Does Vogue *do fashion shoots on campuses? Shoot pictures of models wearing chic twentieth-century clothes in eighteenth-century settings? Must look into this, Diary, but must also control my tendency to follow interesting people out of curiosity. For William & Mary she was interesting.*

10/6/72:

Boldly entered the Brafferton with various papers in hand, pretending to be doing college business. And there she was, sitting behind a desk in an ordinary—if rather fancy—office, to all appearances a sort of receptionist. But she is apparently the new secretary to the provost. I fled, saying I'd lost my way and was in the wrong building. She has a deepish lovely voice.

4/5/73:

The new secretary to the provost and I had lunch again today. A hurried lunch, as she's very busy virtually running the college, as she seems to do, from her post in the Brafferton. I met her husband for the first time. A handsome, smart, biology professor—Italian family. From upstate New York. The two met in Berkeley, California, at the university. He, too, is very well turned out.

9/12/75:

Dinner with the new secretary to the provost and her husband again. I've been fortunate enough to dine fairly regularly with them. They have many friends and are great hosts. Between them, they set a high standard of style and sprezzatura. Not to mention terrific food.

4/5/2008:

I've been honored by being asked to say something at the retirement of my friend and associate, now for many years titled the assistant to the provost. I can't think of what words would be adequate to describe the role she has played here all these years.

How to communicate the charm, the intelligence, and the panache she displayed as William & Mary's assistant to the provost? How to communicate her long hours, her hard work, and the benefit she's been to faculty? She seems to hold the whole place in her hands. The estimate is that she has provided 115,000 hours of service to William & Mary. The story, perhaps apocryphal, is that nothing could begin in the provost's office before noon when she was on vacation in her native California. After noon, she could be phoned to answer that day's list of difficult questions.

5/1/2008:

Huge turnout on the Wren Lawn for the retirement party for the provost's assistant I once viewed as a Vogue *model. Many friends present from many years. Some tears shed. As Hamlet says of his father, we shall not look upon his like again. Well,* her *like again.*

43. A Conversation over Fishing

In the 1970s, when most high executives in the United States were males, a conversation occurred in the unlikely setting of the Canadian province of Ontario. During the conversation, a difference between life at William & Mary and life in the highest echelon of American business world became clear.

During summer vacations, one of William & Mary's professors and his friends often fished for a week at various well-known freshwater fishing holes. One summer, the group fished Lake of the Woods, an island-studded lake that stretches from Minnesota to Ontario to Manitoba. One morning during that week, the professor and a friend from his undergraduate days were talking and casting from their boat. They were anchored in one of the lake's many bays. In the years since both were English majors in college, the friend had risen to become the principal assistant and chief speech writer for the president of a leading Fortune 500 corporation. At that time, his company's annual profits ranked among the top ten corporations in the United States. Some years they ranked as high as second. His was an important job.

While casting among the lily pads, the professor asked, "Is it true that people who work for your corporation *must* wear white shirts and ties to work?"

"Yes, that's true."

"What would happen if someone *insisted* on wearing a blue or striped shirt instead?"

"Well ... a supervisor would come over and tell him quietly that white shirts are required."

"But what if the executive came in the next day *still* wearing a blue or striped shirt?"

"Well, he would be warned again."

"And if he continued to wear colored or striped shirts?"

"We have a branch we have nicknamed 'Siberia.' It is located in a remote area along Lake Ontario. The corporation doesn't fire anyone. We just reassign them to 'Siberia.' And sometimes they quit rather than go."

The casting continued, unrewarded by fish. A few minutes later, the corporate executive had some questions for the professor. "Do you know," he asked, "your president at William & Mary?"

"Well," said the professor, pausing for a minute. "We say hello when we pass on campus. He knows my name. But not much more than that, I guess." After another pause, the professor continued, "Come to think of it, I *did* talk with the president at a faculty buffet this spring. And at some length. I had carried my plate to an empty table. It had a suitcoat draped over one chair. When the suitcoat's owner returned with his plate, I discovered I was sitting next to the president."

"So this was the president's special table?"

"No, no—he sits with the faculty at these buffets. And he would have been relieved that the chair beside him was now occupied. He would have stood out, dining alone at a table."

"So what did you talk about?"

"Well, I actually remember that conversation. I said, 'Hello, Mr. President.'And he replied, using my first name. And then he added, 'I wish you would call *me* by my first name.' I replied that I supposed I should, but that historic colleges usually call their presidents 'Mr.' or 'President,' and that's what I do.

The president responded, 'I appreciate that, but I still hope you will call me by my first name. After all, I call *you* by your first name.'"

The professor continued, "But, you know, the conversation didn't end there. Because as I remember it, I suddenly saw this as an opportunity. So I blurted out, 'And I also don't call you by your first name, Mr. President, because I don't agree with your football policy.'"

The business executive had just cast. At these words, his lure stopped abruptly in midair and plopped into the water. "You said *that* to your president?" the executive asked.

"Sure," the professor replied.

"And what did he say in *return*?" asked the executive.

"Well, as I recall, he said he understood my position."

The professor pulled out a cigar and lit it. The executive shook his head in wonderment. "What did you say then?"

"Nothing. We listened to the luncheon speaker."

44. Ruckus in a Sacred Place

In 2006, the twenty-sixth president of William & Mary dictated a memo about the Christopher Wren Building. The memo directed that the brass cross at the front of the chapel be removed. In a church, the area around the altar that contains numerous compartments is known as the sacristy. The president's memo directed that the chapel staff place the Wren cross in the sacristy but bring it out whenever desired for weddings or services of worship.

The twenty-sixth president of William & Mary was in no way anti-Christian. Born in 1951, he was raised Roman Catholic—and at a time when Roman Catholic churches displayed multiple crosses on their interiors and exteriors. In Williamsburg, the president and his family attended St. Stephen Lutheran Church across from campus. Rather, the president's memo argued that the Wren Chapel should not display a cross, precisely because William & Mary was no longer a church-affiliated college. For 213 years, it had been affiliated with the Church of England or Episcopal Church. But since 1906, it had existed as a state-supported school. And during those one hundred years, the nation, the state, and the student body had changed. At one point, William & Mary's students were overwhelmingly Protestant in background—but no longer. As of 2006 the student body included Christians, Jews, Muslims, Hindus, Buddhists, Sikhs, and students of other or no religious affiliation. The president's memo emerged from his belief that students at a state school should not be obliged to attend lectures and meetings in a chapel dominated by the principal symbol of Christianity.

Apparently, the president consulted few people before he sent this directive out, and that was a big mistake. In college, in academic institutions, and in law schools, he had lived in a secular environment. But the chapel was not a secular building. To his surprise, his memo caused months of controversy, vituperation, and negative national publicity for the school. Most William & Mary faculty supported the change, but the student body, and particularly the alumni, were seriously divided.

Opponents of the cross's removal established a website, www. savethewrencross.org. They secured the signatures of more than 17,000 persons on a petition calling for William & Mary to continue to display the cross in the chapel. Some of these readers were neither students nor alumni, but one alumnus who did sign the petition threatened to withdraw a multimillion-dollar gift to the university if the cross were not returned. The website proclaimed: "A Great University Has to Have a Cross."

"A Great University Has to Have a Cross." Forgetting for a moment about such secular universities as Michigan, Berkeley, Johns Hopkins, and others, the statement was baffling to anyone who knew the history of Christian worship. When the controversy about the cross reached the national media, the director of a national society that studies Christian worship wrote to a William & Mary professor. Before entering the Episcopal clergy, the director had taught English for a decade at William & Mary. His letter to his former colleague expressed concern and bafflement. As a liturgical scholar, he said he could not understand why there was any controversy at all—let alone vitriol—about the removal of the cross. "There never should have been a cross anywhere in the Wren Chapel in the first place," his letter declared.

Why such a dogmatic statement? The scholar wrote those words because he knew that the Wren Chapel had not displayed a cross prior to the year 1937. The chapel was built in 1732; a cross was first placed on its holy table in 1937—that's 205 years without a cross. And so let's look at this vexed question of a cross in the Wren Chapel.

The historical truth is that during all the years that William & Mary was a church-related school, the Wren Chapel had no cross, neither inside nor out. In fact, no Anglican or Episcopal church in Virginia, or Connecticut, or anywhere else in the colonies, had one. From 1777 to 1812, William & Mary's great president, Bishop James Madison, presided over services in the Wren Chapel—but there was no cross present. No founding father—not Washington, or Madison, or Henry—attended an Anglican church that displayed a cross. Colonial Williamsburg and the William & Mary's archives own many photographs of the interior of the Wren Chapel over the years. No photo taken before 1940 has a cross in the picture. All display a plain, unadorned holy table. And that should not surprise us. The Wren Chapel was first built as—and then later reconstructed as— an eighteenth-century Anglican chapel. Anglicans were kind of High Church Protestants, but in the eighteenth century, relatively few Protestant churches anywhere in the world had crosses on their steeples or in their interiors.

Scholars know less about early Christianity and its churches than they would like to know. But it's clear that early Christians worshiped in houses. The earliest church excavated seems to date to the 200s. For safety, it has now been moved from Syria to Yale University. The church was a multiroom house that a Syrian congregation of Christians had adapted into a place of worship. The Syrians added partitions to the church, so that it had four separate rooms or areas: an assembly room, a teaching area, a baptistery, and a courtyard. As far as scholars can tell, it had no sense of sacred or holy space limited to clergy. Like other Christian churches of the time, this house-church contained no cross. In its design, it is reminiscent of a twentieth- or twenty- first-century Evangelical church.

Once Christianity became the state religion of the Roman Empire in the fourth century, its churches became larger and more ornate. Crosses and crucifixes were apparently introduced to churches around 800 or 900, but medieval Christians were initially concerned with keeping crucifixes off the altar. "Let nothing be placed on the altar," a directive repeated several times over the centuries reads, "except relics or the four gospels or the Lord's body."

A significant change occurred in those churches that became Protestant at the time of the Reformation. How is Protestantism defined? A good way is to say that Protestants have attempted to go back to what they believe are original forms of Christian belief and worship. Some Protestant denominations—such as the Mennonites and Baptists—have gone back further into Christian history than others. Hence, under the broad roof of Protestantism, such groups exist as the Evangelicals, Pentecostals, and Mennonites. At the same time, they exist side by side with more formalistic denominations such as the Episcopalians and Lutherans.

Why no crosses in most Protestant churches? The answer is that Reformation Protestants knew from surviving writings that early Christianity did not have crosses in its meeting places. As a result, most Protestant denominations also did not use crosses. The major exception was Lutheranism. After the Reformation, Lutherans largely held on to clerical vestments, structured services, incense, creeds, crosses, and crucifixes.

The leaders of the Reformation were concerned with more than mere imitation. They were also concerned with the way that some Christians made the cross into a kind of idol. Medieval Christians, for example, wore crosses as amulets. They used the cross for healings and for warding off the devil. Some viewed the crucifixes as depicting a living figure and claimed they saw its eyes or limbs move. And Christians also wrote the Apocryphal Gospels—works such as the Gospel of James, the Gospel of Thomas, the Acts of Pilate, and the Gospel of Nicodemus. These spurious gospels might be called "fake Christian news." They depict the cross on which Jesus was crucified, for example, as walking, talking, and performing miracles. Hence, most of the Protestant movement avoided crosses. And sometimes they went to remarkable trouble to do so. In Hungary, for example, the Reformed churches—what English-speaking countries would call "Presbyterian churches"—capped their steeples not with a cross but with a sphere. Spikes protruded from this sphere. These spheres with protruding spikes represented the crown of thorns. It is hard to make a crown of thorns into an idol. Similarly, at the time the Wren Chapel was initially constructed, 1732, non-Lutheran Protestant churches in the American colonies and some Lutheran churches had weathervanes, not crosses, on their steeples.

The liturgist who wrote to the professor during the controversy also expressed surprise that the Evangelical Christians at William & Mary were resisting, not supporting, the removal of a cross from a church. Because, as both the liturgist and the professor knew, Protestant churches did add crosses to their churches in the late nineteenth century. Factions, however, quickly developed. Members who opposed adding a cross to their church's steeple or holy table became known in a church as the "weathervane party." Parishioners who supported a cross being added to their steeple or holy table became known as the "cross party." Generally, the "weathervane party" consisted of Evangelicals. The "cross party" consisted largely of traditionalists. Ironically, the "weathervane party" was generally viewed as the most overtly religious.

The animosity that developed over this issue, on both sides of the ocean, amounted almost to ecclesiastical war-fare. In the Church of England, for example, the weathervane and cross parties actually came to fisticuffs in certain parishes. In the nineteenth century, on some Sundays, Scotland Yard had to be called in to arrest troublemakers and to return peace and quiet during worship. But tensions abounded. And on this side of the ocean, St. Peter's Episcopal Church in Philadelphia was built in 1758 with no cross. But in the late nineteenth century, when its rector wanted to add crosses to its steeple and holy table, his congregation divided bitterly into two parties. Today, St. Peter's Church has a cross, but it was a long haul.

In 1910 in New Jersey, the vestry, or ruling body, of another Episcopal congregation rejected a similar request by its rector. The rector wanted a crucifer carrying a cross to lead the procession of the choir up the aisle every Sunday morning. That is the way Episcopalians worship now, but it wasn't then. The rector reacted indignantly when the vestry refused his request. On the Sunday after the vote, he announced that the service would start with the familiar hymn "Onward Christian Soldiers." But, he said, the congregation would sing new words. Those new words would be:

> *Onward Christian soldiers,*
> *marching as to war.*
> *With the cross of Jesus,*
> *hung behind the door.*

Probably because the South contained more Evangelical churches than the North, churches in the American South were slower to accept crosses than northern churches were. The chapel of the Episcopal Theological Seminary in Alexandria, Virginia, for example, had no cross until the 1960s. In Richmond, the chapel of Union Theological Seminary (a Presbyterian school) lacked a cross until the 1970s. In Williamsburg, Bruton Parish Church got its first cross in 1907, which was early for the South. Yet, churches could be somewhat inconsistent. Williamsburg Baptist Church, for example, had a cross on its communion table— and even an altar boy—in the 1960s. And such anecdotes are common across denominations.

The lack of a cross on the holy table of the Wren Chapel emerged from a theological tradition that dates back to the Reformation and well beyond. Historically, it would seem that no Christian church has to have a cross—because, historically, no Christian church had a cross until about the 800s. If we look at the authoritative Catholic Encyclopedia, it indicates that crucifixes did not become standard on Catholic altars until about the fourteenth century. Scholarship like this prompted Pope John to call a council in 1960 to revise the Catholic liturgy. And so, the Wren Chapel on William & Mary's campus, like some other churches, had no cross in or on it for most of its history. To scholars of liturgy, the furor over the Wren cross was baffling.

In the late 1930s, when W. A. R. Goodwin, the prophet of Colonial Williamsburg, was rector, Bruton Parish Church was being renovated to return the building to more of its eighteenth-century appearance. The renovations caused Bruton's congregation to move out of the church for several years. William & Mary's administration invited Bruton's congregation to worship in the Wren Chapel while construction was going on. Under Goodwin's leadership, Bruton had used a cross on its holy table since 1907. It was the first one Bruton Parish had ever owned. When William & Mary gave permission to worship on Sundays in the Wren Chapel, the congregation brought along their cross. And while these renovations were going on, a donor gave Bruton Parish a new and larger cross to use in its renovated church. When the congregation returned to their church in 1939, they left behind the 1907 cross for the Episcopal students at William & Mary to use in their weekly worship in the Wren Chapel. As an ecumenical gesture, the Canterbury Club left the cross in the Wren Chapel for other denominational groups to use. Protestant denominations were beginning to add crosses to their churches around the year 1940, and from about 1940 on, gradually the cross left in the Wren Chapel became identified as something integral and original to the chapel. To students who entered William & Mary after 1939 or 1940, the Wren cross had always been there.

The furor is baffling because at one time, Evangelicals were the major Protestant opponents of crosses not only in churches but also worn as personal adornment in the US or the British Isles. In fact, even now, some Evangelical churches still do not use crosses. Three major Evangelical colleges—Wheaton, Liberty, and Bob Jones—all reported that they either do not use crosses or else they bring a cross into their chapel only for services of worship. A William & Mary professor who was raised an Evangelical in the Midwest said that he had never seen crosses *on* or *in* an Evangelical church as a boy. He also said he had never seen a cross worn by an Evangelical when he was growing up in the Midwest. Another active Evangelical on the faculty said that no member of his boyhood Southern Baptist church ever wore a cross. Instead, he said, young people wore a mustard seed encased in plastic around their necks, as an allusion to the New Testament parable in which the inconsequential mustard seed grows into a major tree in the kingdom of God. Another Christian who grew up in a heavily Catholic city and his playmates assumed that an adult or child who wore a cross around their neck was Roman Catholic—or some kind of Lutheran.

When did Protestant churches start using crosses on their holy tables or church exteriors? The usage apparently stemmed from the teachings of three British movements in the nineteenth century that worked to "remedievalize" and "unprotestantize" the architecture, worship, and beliefs of the Church of England. Among other things, they emphasized the church building as sacred space—a place where God is viewed as especially present. Church buildings, they taught, should not be just preaching houses, but, rather, places where the appropriate emotion is awe. Many churches, the movements taught, should have certain areas (such as the chancel) where only clergy could go. These three movements also stressed sacred music, mystery, authority, bishops, and the beauty of holiness. And they also emphasized crosses: on churches, in churches, in processions, on robes, in cemeteries, as personal adornment, on rosaries, and the sign of the cross. By the late nineteenth century, the teachings of these three British movements were trickling down and influencing other nations and their churches.

What happened after that? In the 1920s, national denominations began to hire public relations firms to assist in evangelism. One technique involved doing what the German Lutherans in their big cities were already doing after World War I: shining a spotlight at night on a church's steeple. That practice led to the addition of crosses on some steeples. During World War II, soldiers of many Christian backgrounds wore crosses with them into combat. They might not have come from much of a religious background, but war was war. In the 1950s, Pentecostal pastors, led by Oral Roberts, began to bless numerous crosses and send them to radio and TV audiences. And Roman Catholic, Eastern Orthodox, Lutheran, and some Episcopal churches were doing much the same things.

By the 1950s, many Protestant churches were using crosses in some fashion. The Evangelical churches seemed to be the last to have adopted them. The use of the cross seems to have peaked in the 1960s. The cause involved the teachings of the Second Vatican Council. That council, called in 1962 by Pope John XXIII, aimed at returning Catholic churches to earlier forms of Christian worship and architecture. That meant building churches in the round and worshiping in languages other than Latin. It also meant simplifying worship, minimizing ornamentation, and allowing worshipers to receive wine—not just bread—during Mass. The council also meant reducing or removing crucifixes from the altars of Roman Catholic churches. After the council's decision on crosses, church architects in many traditions have downplayed the use of the cross. Many churches have been built in the round, which usually means reducing the sacred space. The exteriors of these post-1960s churches may look like libraries or schools. Most tend to minimize the use of a cross. Inside, they may have a cross suspended from the ceiling or placed to one side of the altar. In a Roman Catholic church, the only crucifix visible near the chancel may be a small one used to lead the procession. All of this is an attempt to return to the worship patterns of early Christianity.

The direction of church architecture often changes. But its direction today is toward churches that serve multiple purposes.

The intention is to place churches at the center of a community's activities throughout the week—just as cathedrals once were. Everything in some churches except the organ, and sometimes even that, is portable. These churches may use simple four-legged tables, not massive carved altars; small podiums, not raised pulpits; and chairs, not pews. Clergy may conduct services from changeable platforms, not from permanent chancels. Churches may even have gymnasiums, as they did in the early twentieth century. In addition, many modern churches are designed to serve as venues for concerts, lectures, recitals, plays, or secular meetings. In other words, they are designed to be *precisely the multipurpose space that the Wren Chapel has long been.* Often these churches have no cross anywhere. At a concert in Williamsburg in St. Bede's Catholic Church, the processional crucifix used during Mass was not on display. Where was it? It was in the sacristy. And that's precisely where the president's memo directed that the Wren cross be kept.

The absence of a cross on the holy table of the Wren Chapel for 205 years was no accident. It emerged from a theological vision that few Christians know or believe in today. In 2006, most who criticized the president's decision knew no other tradition. To worship in a church that did not display a cross seemed strange and even wrong. They were naturally inclined to view the removal of the cross from the Wren Chapel as secular, disrespectful, irreverent, and even sacrilegious. All of those terms were used by opponents during the dispute.

History tells a different story. To remove a twentieth-century cross from an eighteenth-century chapel that lacked a cross for its first two centuries seems neither disrespectful nor irreverent. In the words of L. P. Hartley, "The past is a foreign country: they did things differently there."[1]

What happened to the Wren cross? The removal of the cross caused serious trouble for the twenty-fifth president. Ultimately the president appointed a carefully chosen fourteen-member committee of students, faculty, and alumni who voted unanimously to place the cross and a commemorative plaque in a glass case in a prominent place in the Wren Chapel. A longtime faculty member cochaired the committee. He said it reached its decision after only a few hours of discussion. The mood of the committee, he said, was upbeat and positive throughout. In retrospect, it seems that this controversy need not have happened at all.

45. Eulogy for a Provost

What is it that causes people to automatically like some persons? One of the answers plainly seems to be *calculation*. A person who is not calculating, one who we always know is himself rather than trying to be someone else, is usually quickly accepted into a group of friends.

William & Mary's first provost came to Williamsburg in 1971 under the title of "vice president for academic affairs." It was soon changed to "provost." By whatever name, the provost came as second-in-command to the president of the college. William & Mary's first provost came to Williamsburg from Bates College, a historic liberal-arts college in Maine. He arrived at a time when many faculty themselves were newly arrived in Williamsburg. William & Mary's dean of the faculty, a revered figure and a noted classroom lecturer, had hired many of the professors whom the provost inherited.

Not surprisingly, the provost and the dean of the faculty liked each other. The two men shared many characteristics. What was said of one could equally be said of the other. Faculty might not always agree with their decisions. But they knew that both men always attempted to determine what was right—and then they tried to do it, regardless of personal cost. When professors who served under the provost reminisce today, they tend to repeat certain words—*dedication, decency, tolerance, perseverance, lack of pretension*—and, above all, the words *integrity* and *honor*. Interestingly, many of these reminiscences include praise for the provost's prose style. "He was an outstanding writer," one professor said. "He wrote overwhelmingly convincing memoranda." Another professor called him "elegant—elegant as a writer of correspondence and memos, elegant as a human being." Another spoke of him as "the ultimate honorable gentleman." One professor described him as "a Quaker who never set foot in a Quaker meeting."

As chief academic officer, the provost worked to develop the potential of historic William & Mary while retaining the college's uniqueness and high quality. He deeply believed in the liberal arts and sciences. Because he did, he protected the faculty and students of William & Mary as best he could from the economic and academic realities of the time. Those realities included years of parsimonious general assemblies. They also included years of accepting the direction of governors and boards of visitors appointed by governors who did not necessarily share the liberal-arts values of a historic college. Not until 1983, twelve years after the provost came to William & Mary, did Virginia begin to allocate funding for education in a manner comparable to education-minded states.

A teacher and mentor at heart, William & Mary's first provost knew who he was and what he had in himself to give to America's second-oldest college. He believed in *responsibility*. He did his job as he thought it should be done—without complaint. He did not ask for more resources or help. If that meant that he wrote on a yellow legal pad, used an antique calculator that seemingly dated from the Spanish-American War, and worked in his office in the Brafferton late at night—then so be it. As another administrator said, "He did his work, and his work was generally meticulous, and he took complete responsibility for it."

Thoroughly honorable, the provost was always generous to people with whom he disagreed. He did not deal in condemnatory words or in ad hominem attacks. He did not challenge the good faith of others. After the Golden Decade of Education that stretched from the 1950s to the 1960s ended, college and university faculty tended to be immobile. Today, many end their careers at the same schools where they began decades earlier. That being the case, it is crucial that faculty serve under leaders whom they *trust*. When the longtime provost of Bates College chose to come to William & Mary, professors, students, and alumni were fortunate. They were even more fortunate when he chose to stay. All of which is to say: William & Mary was *lucky*.

46. Education Is a Serious Matter

In 1923, the president of William & Mary persuaded a leading Episcopal minister and author from New York to join the faculty. He charged him with establishing a new department called Biblical Literature and Religious Studies. At this time in American higher education, Protestant or Roman Catholic institutions generally had departments of religion; secular schools did not. The faculties of these early religion departments tended to consist of clergy, dedicated laity, or nuns. On the whole, these colleges viewed their programs in religion as auxiliaries to their religious mission. Beginning in the 1950s and 1960s, the academic study of religion spread to public universities in America. One scholar of religious studies described this new approach as "an insider-outsider" view. "The aim is ... not to understand it from the 'insiders'" perspective," he wrote, "but to analyze and critique it from the outside. We do not try to convert anyone." Since then, many religion departments across the nation have developed in a more secular direction.

In 1967, William & Mary's annual report recommended that a department of religion be added to its curriculum (like most departments of religion, William & Mary's department later adopted the name "Department of Religious Studies"). The then administration at the college supported the recommendation, as did the Board of Visitors. But vigorously opposing it were some senior professors who had taught at William & Mary during the brief existence of a 1920s-era Biblical Literature and Religious Studies department. They viewed the Board of Visitors as having imported flat-earth advocates. "We *do* philosophy. We *do* economics," a highly respected philosopher with William & Mary and Harvard degrees declared in an open meeting of the faculty called to discuss the proposed new department. "Are we now going to *do* religion? And if so, how? What does *doing religion* mean?"

Ultimately, the faculty approved the establishment of a religion department, and the administration appointed a search committee to select a chair of the new department.

After a national search, the scholar ultimately selected to bring the study of religion to William & Mary's campus was a midwesterner raised in an area of the United States settled by conservative Dutch

Protestants in the nineteenth century. Its major city, Grand Rapids, was once described as having "a church—not a bar—on every street corner." Following an excellent academic and athletic grade school and high school in the straitlaced town, the future chairman enrolled in Kenyon College, then a highly selective mid-western college with a reputation of nearly Ivy League stature. Its faculty included leading poets, novelists, and playwrights. It published a prestigious "little magazine" or literary review. The exceptional education the chairman received there shaped the kind of department he later founded at William & Mary. He was essentially an Ivy Leaguer in academic outlook. His models for William & Mary were institutions such as Princeton and Dartmouth. Enrolling after college in one of the premier Protestant theological seminaries in the United States, he studied there with nationally known scholars, just as he had done in college. Ordination as a Presbyterian minister and service as an assistant at leading churches in New York City followed. Subsequently he enrolled in a PhD program in religious studies at an Ivy League university, where again he studied with leading scholars. Later, he became a fellow of Clare College Cambridge and took some of his research sabbaticals there. After finishing his doctorate, he taught at a private university. There he received its outstanding professor award for three successive years. He left to become chair of the Department of Religion at William & Mary.

Insisting on academic rigor, the professor wanted William & Mary's undergraduates to receive an education equal to that offered at the most serious schools in the nation. As for himself, he hoped to become an internationally known scholar. The department established two chairs—one in Divinity and one in Oriental Languages (Hebrew and Greek). As his department grew, he advised new members to pitch their lectures at the same high level they would expect at the most distinguished liberal-arts colleges in the nation. A colleague who sat through a semester of his teaching said that he not only did precisely that but also carried most of his students with him. An alumnus who is himself a professor of religion remembers the chairman's approach to lectures and grading as "meticulous."

In societal affairs, the department head was far from an elitist. He vigorously supported the civil rights movement and in elections almost always voted for the more liberal candidate. But when advisees applied to graduate study, he always directed them to the elite institutions. Many students he advised gained admission to those programs, for at universities such as Harvard, Yale, Chicago, or Oxbridge, a letter of recommendation from William & Mary's leading scholar opened doors.

Yet, for many years the chair's teaching load remained that of an undergraduate professor. Even when William & Mary named him to an endowed chair in religion, his teaching load did not change. Across the nation, the professors known for a steady stream of publications taught four courses fewer a year than he. These professors turned over most, or all, of their grading and some of their lecturing to the graduate students who served as their teaching assistants. Despite the high teaching load, the chair published as frequently as leading scholars. His intellectual achievement as a scholar was nothing less than remarkable. From 1967 until his death in 2011, he authored seven books and edited four. One remained available through fifteen printings, three went into second editions, and one was republished five times. Professors at colleges and universities throughout the nation and overseas adopted his textbooks. He regularly won prestigious national awards and fellowships. In religious studies circles, he became a well-known figure.

Despite his dedication to research, the chairman never lost his focus on undergraduate education. A colleague remembers when a student knocked on his office door late one afternoon and said that the professor was already ten minutes late for their appointment.

Had anyone seen him? The colleague replied that the professor was never late for appointments and that something must have delayed him. Just then, both parties heard big bouncing steps coming down the hall. The professor apologized profusely to the student. He was plainly embarrassed, thinking his lateness made it appear he was indifferent toward his undergraduate students.

During his career, the professor served on almost forty William & Mary committees, chairing ten, most of which dealt with undergraduate education. He remained far more interested in contributing to a top-quality undergraduate education than in educating graduate students. He once told a colleague, "The last thing we need in this department is a graduate program."

As the years went on, departments of religious studies across the nation became increasingly secular. But the leading scholar of William & Mary's religion department remained unembarrassed by his religious beliefs. He did not proselytize, but in conversations he could and would defend the Judeo-Christian tradition rationally. A member of the physics department remembers that when he questioned one particular Judeo-Christian doctrine in a conversation, the chairman not only defended it but also went to the library and brought back the best book on the topic. His publications and classroom lectures probed deeply. Readers and William & Mary students knew where the founder of William & Mary's religious studies department stood. For him, liberal-arts education and religion were serious matters.

47. Pathfinder

He arrived in 1980 after having served as dean of admissions at Ohio Wesleyan University. At William & Mary, he followed a dean of admission who had served the college for twenty years. Staff will say that twenty years is a long time for a dean of admissions to serve. Every year, admissions officers do the same things. Applications go out. Applicants send completed ones back. Admissions staff review the applications. The dean signs offers to selected applicants.

Dean: *In admissions, the word "yield" specifies the percentage of students who enroll after acceptance. Normally the average yield our office at William & Mary expected was around 50 to 52 percent. But in the* *mid-1980s, the yield fell to 49 percent. Then two years later, it fell to 46 percent. A trend line seemed to be emerging. So we took a second look at the year's applicants and emerged with a new estimated yield in the 45 to 46 percent range for the next academic year. That estimate meant that the dean needed to extend more offers to high school seniors. The last thing an admissions dean wants is to be forced in the summer to fill freshmen seats for the fall. And so we extended more offers.*

Every April, William & Mary holds an open house to give potential applicants a chance to tour the campus and to meet with enrolled students and faculty. When the president of William & Mary spoke at the reception, the freshmen apparently were impressed. In any case, the yield went back up to 51 or 52 percent. As a result, William & Mary had way too many students in the freshman class—something like 100 to 150.

What to do? The Office of Student Affairs took over. Somehow they found places for every one of those excess students. I was surprised. At most schools, if you went over your quota by that much, it meant double rooms were going to become triples, single beds became bunk beds, etc. In sum, it was going to be a hassle.

The nine years of my tenure here as admissions dean were comfortable. One disadvantage was that staff was small; the admissions office had more clerical than professional staff. Now that ratio is the other way around. Today, admissions has a lot more professional staff than it did in our day. During my deanship, we would usually accept one out of every four applicants—or roughly 25 percent. The yield would then be about 50 percent.

Today, if I understand correctly, those numbers are reversed. Colleges and universities admit one out of two, and their yield is one out of four. That's in part because today's computer-savvy students can easily fill out more admission applications. Each college no longer has its own separate hard copy. Schools now use the common application. Students fill it out only once online. After submitting fees, they can then apply to any number of colleges. And families who are worried that their child won't get into any college allow their children to apply to many schools. As a result, admissions offices receive far too many applications, causing the estimates of yields to be inaccurate.

Interviewer: *This book covers 1950–2000. I'm reminded that you stopped me once on the campus years ago. It may have been the year after we hosted the Ford-Carter presidential debate and gained national attention. You said, "There's blood on the floor in the admissions office today." Now there's a phrase I hadn't heard before, and I was a bit shocked. Then you said, "All these good applicants that we don't have room for, and we're cutting them."*

Dean: *Oh yes, it was so painful. And so you start off on the ends. There are obviously people on the right end that are so good you have to admit them, and there are people on the left end that need to look for another college. But when you get to the big middle, where everyone looks alike on paper—their numbers are similar. So now it becomes highly subjective. The questions we ask become: Did their voice come through on their essay? Do they appear to be someone whom we've never had before, someone whom the professors will find interesting to teach? You get into questions like that. You're not just choosing interesting people, but you're also choosing alumni who will do wonderful things someday.*

Interviewer: *I've always felt that way about William & Mary students. You should see this book. It's filled with achievement.*

Dean: *I remember especially a young man from Orrville, Ohio. His father, who ran a large family business there, spoke at the business school. He had brought his wife, and they discovered William & Mary. At the time, their son was a junior in high school. They said to me, "Our son would probably enjoy coming to a place like this—if we can make it happen." So I asked a colleague in the business school if he had a few minutes to talk with the parents. He did. He sat down with us, and we talked about the college. When the couple left, they said, "You may hear from us again." We did, and some of us got to know the family when their son attended William & Mary.*

I was invited to speak at their local high school. When the parents invited me to their home for dinner, I got to meet a real midwestern American family. They had been in business since the first day that the grandfather started putting jelly in jars.

Fast-forward to today. After graduating from William & Mary, the son went to work for the family company; he is now its CEO. To this day we still have contact. When I was ill earlier this year, the father called.

At William & Mary I started some initiatives to assist the admissions process. I started a summer program named Discovery that brought high school rising seniors and had them stay on campus for a week. They learned a lot about the college admissions process. And to help them, I established a faculty of college deans and highly rated secondary-school college placement counselors to teach. After a week of "brain camp," the kids all came home very prepared to run the process of applying to college in the fall themselves. Their parents didn't need to remind them of what needed to be done. Even though I haven't had a summer program for several decades, I still hear good comments about Discovery.

Interviewer: *Well, I know this, because two of my kids went through the program.*

Dean: *We also, at that time, became involved in the evaluation of transfer applicants, which had not been a part of the undergraduate admissions program. We took on a number of responsibilities such as these with a very small professional staff.*

Interviewer: *And initially a very small office.*

Dean: *Yes, we were stuffed into half of the Ewell suite of offices. I was able to move us into the old president's office in Ewell. Beautiful—the nicest office I've ever had. Unfortunately, other people wanted it too. After nine years at William & Mary, I became headmaster of a highly regarded preparatory school in Grosse Pointe, Michigan. If I had stayed at William & Mary instead of accepting that offer, the department would probably have been moved into a broom closet. It took some years for William & Mary to learn that its interests were well served if we recruited out of state.*

Interviewer: *Did you have any great surprises or shocks that occurred when you were dean of admissions?*

Dean: *Well, as I said, my background was in northwestern Pennsylvania and Ohio. I attended a small undergraduate liberal-arts college.*

Interviewer: *You went to Colgate?*

Dean: *Yes, Colgate. Originally a men's college. Set in the middle of nowhere, sitting on top of a hill. I used to say, "In Hamilton, New York, there's only one stoplight, and we use it for driver education." That's one of my jokes.*

William & Mary was my first taste of being a state employee. So early on, I had a few run-ins about expense accounts and things like that. There were a lot of rules imposed by the Virginia legislature about how you could spend taxpayer money as part of your job.

Interviewer: *No booze.*

Dean: *No booze, and the state would not pay for lunch for college guests if you bought it within 30 miles of your house. At one point, a disgruntled clerical admissions employee retired and went to a local newspaper and reported that I was abusing state money for lunch. I had a practice where, if a high school counselor was in town, I'd walk them over to the Trellis restaurant and buy them a sandwich or something. Later I'd turn in that bill as an expense. Well, using the Freedom of Information Act, the newspaper subpoenaed all my expense accounts and financial statements. Our business office only had so many days to review them before they had to turn these materials in. They found only one impropriety. The business office told me if I wrote a check to cover that charge, then I'd be clear. So, I did, and I never heard anything more from that newspaper. It goes to show that anytime you are in a new place, you meet a lot of people who think the status quo is divine, and don't like changes.*

When I got here, I had an attitude about military children. I hadn't known many. But I had always thought what a horrible, horrible experience for children to be dragged all over the world, moving every year or two because of their parents' career in the military. In this part of the world, the Defense Department is extremely well known. I was told once that within an hour of Williamsburg, there are seventy-two military institutions of one form or another. Anyhow, in Virginia I found the most interesting kids to talk to were the military dependents. That is, the kids who had to pick up and adjust to moving all the time, to constantly make new friends, and to become comfortable with new adults. These kids, I came to think, had a tremendous advantage in life because they had been to so many places.

Interviewer: *What was your attempt to increase the number of states from which William & Mary received applications?*

Dean: *I thought diversity in any form is desirable. Admissions did more out-of-state travel for William & Mary than I think had been done in the past.*

Interviewer: *Oh yes. Much more, and it brought us some splendid students.*

Dean: *Well, there were the exceptions. I remember we used to need permission to drive a state car out of state. Not until my third year did state cars actually come with radios in them. It was the 1980s, long before cars had GPS. We did look for applicants that came from farther away. In those days, William & Mary always had a few star students that came to us from out of state. As much as Virginia citizens respected William & Mary's prestige in-state, we had never really been given the go-ahead to allow that prestige to spread. William & Mary was not well known outside Virginia—it was a big secret.*

In fact, when I was on the admissions staff at Bucknell University, I interviewed a Virginia female who I thought was an excellent candidate. In the course of our conversation, I asked what other colleges she was considering. She mentioned William & Mary as one. I said, "Well, if you got into all of them, where do you think you might want to go?" She said, "William & Mary because it's so much cheaper than all those other colleges." That's when I said to my boss at Bucknell, "Why would they be so much cheaper? William & Mary is just another college, right?" Well, my boss, the dean of admissions, didn't realize that William & Mary was a state university. Today you can still go out to certain hinterlands of Virginia, and you'll meet people that don't know William & Mary is part of the state system. The name makes people think we're a private or religious school.

One day I got a telephone call from a man who had been the dean of admissions at three highly respected American schools. He was a writer—a good writer. At that time, he was working on a book that eventually became known as The Public Ivies.

Interviewer: *Yes, we all knew that book.*

Dean: *He called me one day and said, "I'm at the University of Virginia writing a book about state universities that are very much as selective as some of the best private colleges in the country. Do you think I could come down and stay in your area, meet students and people, and then do a chapter in the book on William & Mary?"*

We put him up for three days. When he got to Williamsburg, this man who later became known as the absolute *expert on selective state universities confessed that he compiled a list of colleges that were going to be in the book, and that William & Mary was not on that list. The book included chapters on five state universities from Vermont to Michigan. The author spent a couple of days in Charlottesville with a dean who later became a college president. As he was getting ready to leave Charlottesville, the dean asked, "I guess your next stop will be William & Mary?"*

"No," the author said. "I'm only doing state universities." Because he had become the guru of high-quality state universities, he denied he ever said that. But when he finished the book, I think he wound up saying, "William & Mary—of all the places I've been, of all the people I've met, I think William & Mary has the most impressive and probably the best state university in the country."

Interviewer: *We haven't discussed that you were at Ohio Wesleyan before you came to William & Mary.*

Dean: *Yes, until 1975 I was at Bucknell. I wasn't looking for another job. But a telephone call came from Ohio Wesleyan. They explained that they had advertised for a director of admissions in the* Chronicle of Higher Education. *A good group of applicants had applied. During their search, the committee consulted with high school counselors and ran the names of the nominees past them. At one historic preparatory school, the dean of students listened to the list of applicants and said, "There's one name missing from your list" (and he gave them my name). And so the search committee added me to their conversation and then, even though I never applied, put my name on the list for director of admissions. For some reason, everybody the committee then called said that I was the man. When I received an invitation to interview from Ohio Wesleyan, the job was mine to lose. I interviewed and accepted. My bride and I moved to Delaware, Ohio.*

I had four years at that fine institution. In my third year, I started part-time on a PhD at Ohio State. I was given a good research position there, and I was free to look for other jobs. And that's how William & Mary happened.

Interviewer: *One time when we had dinner, I recall your saying, "Well, I guess my successor at Ohio Wesleyan would about be going home now, having made his last telephone call." It was 8 p.m. when you made that statement.*

Dean: *Oh, yes, that was a different kind of job. It was night and day from the job at William & Mary.* Selection *and* recruitment *were the keys. Each year we had to find enough bodies to pay the light bill, and that was a different job.*

When I was at Ohio Wesleyan, my counterpart at Kenyon College was a great friend. We had occasional meetings and lunches. Anyhow, he worked as hard as I did. I could be at my desk Sunday afternoon and could pick up the phone and call him in Gambier and he'd be at his desk. Whenever we talked, we'd say how much we loved our jobs and what a great job we held.

I went on a trip to Puerto Rico. When I came back, my friend was in the hospital with a heart attack. I rushed over to the hospital. In his room, he said, "We were wrong. We shouldn't work this hard." He died about two years later when his heart finally gave out.

Interviewer: *Another question. To whom did William & Mary constantly lose students?*

Dean: *I think we only had one challenge, and that was from the University of Virginia—and that was for male students. Every year I could almost predict, to within five persons, the number of applicants that we would receive from in-state males. So, UVA was our only competition.*

In my current education, I've learned that the best educational institution is probably a little one-teacher, one-room schoolhouse in, say, Montana. Just a little building where the older kids help the younger kids and where those seven or eight kids would have the teacher's undivided attention all day. After that, the more you add to the number of students, the more I think the decline in quality becomes self-evident. Colgate had 1,300 men.

Interviewer: *It would be larger now.*

Dean: *Yes, enrollment is three thousand now. But most of those were women added when the college went coed. In my case, I had been recruited as a football player, and I had no idea what I was doing at Colgate. I would get an occasional call from the secretary to the dean of students. She would ask me to come in and talk to the dean about how I was doing in classes. One day, I said, "I'm a little worried about that biology class that we all have to take. I have no idea what's happening in there." And the dean said, "I'll take care of it." I didn't know what he meant. Well, about three days later a premed student knocked on my dorm room door and said, "The dean sent me to tutor you in biology." So that's the way he took care of it. That was my idea of the ideal college for a bum like me, an immature kid from the coal-mining and steel mill area of western Pennsylvania. I am eating this up, talking about myself.*

48. The Chancellor's Speech

The Royal Charter of 1693 specifies that the College of William & Mary shall have a chancellor. During the colonial period, Anglican bishops—generally bishops of London—served as chancellors. Their role was largely honorary and ceremonial. None ever visited the American colonies. After the colonies separated from England in 1776, prominent figures—including George Washington, Prime Minister Margaret Thatcher, and US Secretary of State Henry Kissinger—held the position.

During the investiture of Supreme Court Justice Sandra Day O'Connor as the twenty-third chancellor of William & Mary in 2006, an incident occurred that caused great secret merriment. The setting was the back portico, or porch, of the Christopher Wren Building on a glorious Williamsburg day. The attending members of the Board of Visitors sat in chairs surrounding the steps to the Wren portico. The large audience was seated in rows of chairs extending toward the Sunken Garden. To stay hydrated in heavy robes under the Friday afternoon sun, many of the official party carried plastic bottles of water with them to the stage, hiding their bottles beneath ceremonial robes.

During the long ceremony, the twenty-sixth president of William & Mary examined the role public education plays in addressing the ills of society. The William & Mary choir sang with exuberance. A few students spoke and spoke well. Then the time arrived for the new chancellor to speak. In her talk, Justice O'Connor expressed delight at becoming part of the centuries-old William & Mary family. The holder of undergraduate and law degrees from Stanford University, she described what education had done for her and for many other people.

While Justice O'Connor was speaking, a new member of the Board of Visitors—a 1973 graduate of William & Mary—felt an elbow in his right side. The elbow belonged to a major benefactor and board member seated on the right of the new board member. He described her by saying, "Few alumni are more devoted to the college."

The experienced board member had spotted a plastic bottle lying on the stairs, directly in the path of the chancellor. The veteran member feared that the new chancellor could trip over the bottle and tumble down the steps and would be seriously hurt. Even if she were uninjured, a photograph or video of her fall would surely lead the news that evening and top her investiture as William & Mary's chancellor. If the chancellor's injuries were serious enough to require hospitalization, the campus would be deluged with reporters in the next days. All institutions of higher learning want publicity, but not of this kind.

Because of the disaster that could lie ahead, the experienced board member had nudged the new member to get his attention. In a whisper, speaking almost out of the side of her mouth, she directed him to go out to the brick path. Halfway up the Wren steps, she said, he would find a stray water bottle in the path of the new chancellor. She pointed it out and instructed him to retrieve it. She also insisted that the new member—a former William & Mary basketball player, 6 foot 7 in height and 230 pounds in weight—must crawl to the bottle. Otherwise, she whispered, his body would block the television cameras covering the investiture. He must not replace Justice O'Connor as the focus of the ceremony.

The new board member listened with amazement. Going out and retrieving the errant bottle was one thing—but crawling to do so was another. Asked in later years why he didn't simply refuse to crawl, he explained that the senior board member was highly experienced in academic ceremonies, and he respected her judgment. Seeing no other options, he slid carefully off his chair, dropped to his knees, and began to crawl toward the Wren steps.

"I discovered," he later reflected, "that crawling on my knees in a full-length robe ... was most cumbersome. The robe severely restricted how far each knee could move forward. In effect, I inched forward. It was like trying to walk with the laces of my tennis shoes each tied to the other foot. It reminded me of when, as a sophomore on the William & Mary basketball team, I tried to guard a lightning-quick All-American forward for UCLA. My legs and arms moved with neither enough coordination nor enough speed."

The board member crawling on all fours smack dab in the middle of the chancellor's speech quickly became the center of attention. Posterity has not recorded how many members of the audience exchanged mystified looks. Known for her unflappability, Chancellor O'Connor—who had to have seen the crawling man— gave no indication that she had.

Finally, the tall drink of water extended his long, basketball player arm. He nabbed the offending plastic bottle. Trying hard not to detract from the solemnity of the occasion, he inched backward—a difficult maneuver even without robes—toward his seat. When reseated, he stowed the bottle under his chair.

Turning to the veteran board member and future mentor beside him, he whispered, "They never told me that saving the chancellor from hazardous water bottles would be one of my responsibilities as a board member."

Hearing of this incident for the first time, one staff member said, "If I had been there, I would've found it very difficult not to burst out laughing. I mean, imagine a 6 foot 7 man weighing who knows what crawling on the ground in full regalia during a ceremonial occasion." Others wondered if this investiture was a production of the department of comedy. But most asked, "What were they drinking?"

V. CONCLUSION

49. Changes Bring Inclusion

Diversification—the act of increasing variety—has a strong recent history at William & Mary. Like other early American colleges, it was founded as a school to train male clergy and to educate sons of the landed gentry in the liberal arts. The students were white—a composition that remained until the early twentieth century.

Women were the initial addition. In the 1918–1919 academic year, William & Mary became the first coeducational college in Virginia by admitting twenty-four women. In the same year, the college also added three women faculty. By 1929, women composed almost 41 percent of the student body. By 1934, they were one-third of the faculty.[1] For various reasons, the percentage of women faculty then dropped. Through the 1980s, it averaged around 12 percent of the faculty. Toward the end of the century, the active pursuit of qualified woman raised it to about 45 percent. In 2018, one hundred years after the first woman was admitted, William & Mary appointed its first female president, Katherine Rowe.

As the twentieth century progressed, representatives of other races and cultures gradually joined William & Mary as students and faculty. In the 1920s, a student of Chinese descent received an AB degree. Five years later, a Japanese American not only earned a bachelor's degree but also distinguished himself on the football field. The entering class of 1933 included the first female of Asian descent. In 1948, a new instructor in government became the university's first known Asian American faculty member. Another Asian American, raised in an Arkansas internment camp for Japanese during World War II, made significant contribution to the Department of Sociology.

During the mid-1950s, the Supreme Court decision in *Brown v. Board of Education* declared segregation in public schools unconstitutional. In that decade, William & Mary admitted two African American men for postgraduate work and one African American woman to its law school. In the same decade, a Black faculty member came to William & Mary from Hampton Institute to teach English to Japanese exchange students.

The 1960s saw the admissions of the first Black undergraduates as well as the first Black residents in William & Mary dorms. According to one, their undergraduate experiences were "uneventful compared to desegregation at other predominately white colleges." By the end of the decade, Black and sympathetic white students established the Black Student Organization.

From the 1970s through 2000, William & Mary's campus became increasingly diverse. In 1972, the Order of the White Jacket was founded to recognize William & Mary undergraduates who worked in food service. During the same year, the Title IX Educational Amendment caused the growth of women's sports programs on campus. Also in that year, the Department of Anthropology hired the first African American professor. In 1974, the Office of Minority Affairs (later renamed the Center for Student Inclusion and Diversity) was created. Phi Beta Kappa (as a vignette in this book indicates) inducted the first of many African American members in 1978.

Two years later, William & Mary established the position of dean of Multicultural Affairs. Later that decade, students founded the Korean American Students Association, and faculty and alumni established GALA, the first support group for gay and lesbian students.

The 1990s saw the founding of the Indian Cultural Association and the Filipino-American Student Association. In 1993, Hillel, the largest Jewish campus organization, came to William & Mary. In February of 2018, ground was broken for the Shenkman Jewish Center. The university added sexual orientation to its nondiscrimination clause. Multicultural and interdisciplinary faculty members worked together to develop the Black Studies Program.

These events provide only a sampling of the employment, admissions, and organizations that brought greater diversity to William & Mary during the last half of the twentieth century. Ahead lay the Lemon Project, which acknowledged the legacy of slave ownership and systemic racism at William & Mary. Lemon was the previously unknown African American slave who worked for the college. A second project would focus on the Brafferton Indian School. By

2020, William & Mary listed more than 450 student groups, thirty-nine of which are related to culture and identity.

The second-oldest college in the United States may have begun as a school for Anglican clergy and white gentry, but by the end of the twentieth century it had become a diverse university.

50. From Sputnik to Vietnam and Beyond

After the three students referenced in the first chapter graduated, many things changed at William & Mary. As the 1950s moved into the 1960s, changes—often radical— occurred on most college campuses in America. Classes that graduated in the later 1960s and early 1970s entered college as a part of the earnest Sputnik generation; however, by graduation they were transitioning into the Vietnam era. The 1960s were characterized by increased funding for faculty, facilities, and research. During those years, student unrest began to occur. Across the nation, students demonstrated over civil rights, political activism, and a war in a former French colony, which took more than 58,000 American lives. Having contemporaries who were drafted to Vietnam or who fled to Canada to escape the draft made students demand to be treated more as adults. If an eighteen-year-old could be drafted, they argued, he or she should have the right to determine college behavior. Across the nation, these protests gradually turned violent. Unrest increased after the Ohio National Guard shot thirteen students at Kent State University in 1970.

At William & Mary, protests remained peaceful, but students rallied to ask for reform of rules pertaining to visiting the opposite sex, having cars on campus, drinking, and the dress code. The college newspaper, the *Flat Hat*, called for sweeping changes, especially of parietal regulations. Persons aware of the level of protests on other campuses considered William & Mary tame by contrast. A member of the physics department who previously had taught in the University of California system was stunned that Virginia newspapers treated William & Mary as a center of political radicalism.

In 1971, what was called "the Golden Decade" of expanded funding for higher education ended. At William & Mary, the eleven-year presidency of a Virginia native and former state superintendent of schools ended. The fourteen-year presidency of a Harvard- and Yale-educated Connecticut native began. And life at William & Mary changed.

Year after year during this period, college costs increased, but they were sometimes offset by low-interest loans, grants, and work-study programs. As enrollment grew, the campus in Williamsburg expanded; a new campus was constructed adjacent to the existing campus. William & Mary added graduate programs and separate schools, such as education and business. In 1968, the State Council of Higher Education officially dubbed William & Mary a "modern university."

Curriculum reform led to such interdisciplinary departments as American Studies. Computers became commonplace, and the university added a Department of Computer Science. By the last decades of the century, fax machines, emails, and cell phones had replaced the traditional forms of campus communication.

Not entirely shedding its past, William & Mary continued to feel athletic tension, with various issues and scandals occurring into the twenty-first century. In 1980, the Board of Visitors wished to expand its football stadium (from seating 15,000 to 35,000) so that the university could continue to play national football powers. The faculty and staff voted overwhelmingly against it and forced its academic department to hold a moderate position on football and basketball. In 2020, tensions erupted again when William & Mary's athletic director resigned after students and faculty overwhelmingly opposed her decision to drop seven minor sports from university sponsorship. Big-time athletics have a distinct effect on academic values, but the authors of college and university guides rarely take such matters into consideration when they evaluate colleges for parents and students. For a more accurate viewpoint, they should.

During these transitional decades, diversity of race, ethnicity, and sexual orientation grew at William & Mary. Ahead lay the transition to an increasingly internationalized curriculum and perspective. Curfews and house mothers disappeared. Coed dorms were introduced at many colleges, including William & Mary, but the changes were not without controversy. After the Board of Visitors approved coed dorms, William & Mary's dean of the Undergraduate Program had to get to his office at least by 7 a.m., because promptly at eight o'clock in the morning—and often earlier—he was besieged with telephone calls of protest from parents whose children had chosen to live in a coed dorm. Students now could live off campus. Juniors and seniors could have cars on campus, the women's curfew and dress codes ended, and the administration relaxed penalties for cutting classes.

In the same decades, campus organizations formed at William & Mary that reflected the new student diversity. The vignette "Changes Bring Inclusion" names many of these groups. The university also began to recruit students from a wider geographical area. Enrollment in both undergraduate and graduate programs increased, going from 4,531 in 1971 to 6,640 in 1981. By 2020, undergraduate enrollment stood at 6,285, with graduate enrollment at 2,455. Notable students in the twentieth century included actress Glenn Close, television personality Jon Stewart, Secretary of Defense Robert Gates, and designer Perry Ellis.

The fifty years from 1950 to 2000 brought many changes to American colleges in general and to William & Mary in particular. But the undergraduate teaching excellence and faculty-student interactions remembered by the three alumni and illustrated by the previous vignettes remained central to the essence of the university.

Today's school continues this trend. In 2020, William & Mary offered twenty-five areas of undergraduate specialization, twelve master's programs, and six doctoral programs. Magazines such as *US News and World Report*, *Washington Monthly*, and the *Princeton Review* all rate William & Mary highly in their various rankings. The small college founded for "an hundred scholars more or less"[1] has come of age.

NOTES

Introduction

1. Philippe Lejeune, Annette Tomarken, and Edward Tomarken, "Autobiography in the Third Person," *New Literary History* 9, no. 1 (1977): 27–50, https://doi.org/10.2307/468435.

1. Three Alumni and Life at William & Mary

1. Royal Charter Collection, Special Collections Research Center, Earl Gregg Swem Library, College of William and Mary.

2. Nick Cipolla, "Feature: Scandal and Secrecy," *Flat Hat*, April 5, 2016, https://flathatnews.com/2016/04/05/1951-football-scandal/.

35. Women in a STEM World

1. Patsy Parker, "The Historical Role of Women in Higher Education," *Administrative Issues Journal: Connecting Education, Practice, and Research* 5, no. 1 (Spring 2015): 3–14.

44. Ruckus in a Sacred Place

1. L. P. Hartley, *The Go-Between* (London: Hamish Hamilton, 1953).

49. Changes Bring Inclusion

1. Carolyn Lamb Sparks Whittenburg, "President J. A. C. Chandler and the First Women Faculty at the College of William & Mary," PhD dissertation, William & Mary, 2004.

50. From Sputnik to Vietnam and Beyond

1. Royal Charter Collection, Special Collections Research Center, Earl Gregg Swem Library, College of William and Mary.

BIBLIOGRAPHY

Godson, Susan H., Ludwell H. Johnson, Richard B. Sherman, et al. *The College of William & Mary: A History.* 2 vols. Williamsburg, VA: King and Queen, 1994.

Kale, Wilford. *Hark upon the Gale: An Illustrated History of the College of William & Mary.* Williamsburg, VA: Botetourt, 2007.

McLendon, Jacquelyn Y. *Building on the Legacy: African Americans at William & Mary.* Brookfield, MO: Donning, 2019.

Mohr, Clarence L. *The New Encyclopedia of Southern Culture.* Vol. 17, Education. Chapel Hill: University of North Carolina Press, 2011.

Parker, Patsy. "The Historical Role of Women in Higher Education." *Administrative Issues Journal: Connecting Education, Practice and Research,* no. 1 (Spring 2015): 3-14.

ACKNOWLEDGMENTS

Without the stories, suggestions, research, and advice of the following people, this book would not exist. I am extremely grateful for the time and effort they have spent, allowing me to compile the story of life at William & Mary in the last half of the twentieth century.

I apologize for any errors or omissions in the stories or in this list; the will is strong, but the memory wanes.

My wife, Carolyn, and daughters, Henley and Catesby, encourage me by sparking joy and supporting me with love and patience. They are the light by which I write.

In keeping with my mostly anonymous vignettes, the following list is not organized by chapter, but I would be remiss not to mention your name.

Thank you. David L. Holmes.

For final editing, research, and organization: Susan Williamson.

Assisted by Bill Harris.

For illustrations that greatly enhance the vignettes: David Loebman.

Christopher Abelt, Shirley Aceto, Virginia Alder, Alan F. Albert, Betsy Ballenger, Bruce C. Beringer, Brian Blount, Harold Britenburg, Warren W. Buck III, Michael Chesson, Clayton M. Clemmons, James Cobb, Evan M. Cook, Frederick Corney, Jeffrey Cronin, John C. Dann, Catherine Dann, Don Darden, William F. Davis Jr., Gary C. DeFotis, James Doughat, Kevin S. Doyle, Morton Eckhause, Jack D. Edwards, Enrico Edraden, Judith Ewell, Anne Foster, John W. Frece, Philip J. Funigielio, Armand J. Galpho, Gregory J. Galpho, Duane E. Gerenser, Jerome K. Giles, Amy Goldberg, George Greenia, Bill Harris, Erik W. Haug, Kristin A. Hayes, Thomas L. Heacox, P. Warren Heeman, Louis A. Heilbron, David Hein, R. Lynn Howell, Dudley Jenson, Dale A. Johnson, Louise L. Kale, Richard L. Kiefer, Laura Lee Kostel, Stephen Kohlhagen, Jarret Knight, David E. Kranbuehl, Michael J. Lansing, Nick Lucketti, Robert P. Maccubbin, John C. Marsh, Colleen Murphy McCann, John J. McGlennon, Terry L. Meyers, Robert B. Mullin, Wistar Murray, Charles Nickerson, Ben Noble, Carol Shewmaker O'Connell, Richard H. Palmer, Linda Patchel, Gary Ripple, Shirley G. Roby, Hugh C. Rowland, W. Samuel Sadler, Ito Satoshi, Leonard G. Schifrin, Karen Kennedy Schultz, Carol W. Sherman, Paul Showalter, Leigh Smith, Timothy J. Sullivan, Andrew B. Terry, Jane K. Terry, Roy M. Terry, Elaine M. Themo, David W. Thompson, Steve A. Tuttle, Jeffrey Trammell, Daniel Vaca, Julia Vaca, Stewart A. Ware, Robert E. Welsh, Joseph Wheeless, Brian Whitson, Claire Whittaker, Missy Wycinsky, and Sibel Zardi-Sayek.